Virgil A. Walker

Who is Israel?: A Historic Reflection of Church History

Written by Virgil A. Walker

Published by House Walker Publishing

Who is Israel?: A Historic Reflection of Church History

Published by House Walker Publishing

Copyright © 2025 Virgil A. Walker

All rights reserved. No part of this publication may be reproduced, distributed, or transmitted in any form or by any means, including photocopying, recording, or other electronic or mechanical methods, without the prior written permission of the author, except in the case of brief quotations embodied in critical reviews and certain other noncommercial uses permitted by copyright law.

Virgil A. Walker

Introduction: Defining the True Israel............................4
Chapter 1: The Identity of Israel in the Old Testament 7
Chapter 2: The Coming of Christ and the Continuation of Israel..19
Chapter 3: The Early Church Understanding of Israel 27
Chapter 4: The Historic Church as Israel....................51
Chapter 5: John Darby and the Rise of Dispensationalism 65
Conclusion: Reclaiming the True Israel......................82
Call to Action..92
About the Author 93
Glossary 94
Bibliography 99

Introduction: Defining the True Israel

Who is Israel? This question lies at the heart of Christian theology, shaping how believers understand their identity, God's covenant, and the unfolding of His redemptive plan. For centuries, Christians have grappled with the meaning of "Israel," a term rooted in the promises of the Old Testament and transformed through the coming of Jesus Christ. Is Israel merely a nation, defined by geography and ethnicity, or is it something more—a spiritual community bound by faith in God's promises? This book contends that the True Israel is the Church, the universal body of believers in Christ, and that this understanding is firmly grounded in both Scripture and the historic teachings of the Christian faith.

The idea that the Church is the True Israel is not a modern invention but a conviction held by the early church fathers, medieval theologians, and Reformers alike. From the New Testament's bold proclamation that God's covenant now embraces all who trust in Christ (Galatians 3:28-29) to the writings of figures like Augustine and Calvin, the Church has long been recognized as the heir of God's promises to Israel. This view, rooted in the unity of God's redemptive plan, sees the Church as the fulfillment of the covenant, transcending national boundaries to include all people—Jew and Gentile—united in faith.

Yet, in the 19th century, a new theological perspective emerged that challenged this historic consensus. Dispensationalism, pioneered by John Nelson Darby, introduced a sharp distinction between Israel and the Church, treating them as separate entities in God's plan. This minority view, while not representative of the broader Christian tradition, has gained significant traction, particularly among modern evangelicals. Through influential works like the Scofield Reference Bible and the rise of Christian Zionism, dispensationalism has shaped not only theology but also politics and media, often aligning Christian support with the modern secular state of Israel. This shift has led to a widespread misrepresentation of what Christians have historically believed about Israel, obscuring the Church's identity as the True Israel and fostering division within the body of Christ.

The goal of this book is to reclaim the biblical and historical understanding of Israel as the Church. By tracing the concept of Israel from its Old Testament origins through the transformative work of Christ, the teachings of the early church, and the consistent theology of the historic Church, we will demonstrate that God's covenant people are defined by faith, not by national or ethnic boundaries. We will also examine the rise of dispensationalism, exploring how its novel interpretations have reshaped evangelical thought and contributed to theological confusion. In doing so, we aim to offer a corrective to the distortions of dispensationalism, inviting

Christians to rediscover their true identity as the covenant people of God.

This book is structured to guide readers through this theological journey. Chapter 1 explores the multifaceted identity of Israel in the Old Testament, examining whether it is primarily a nation or a people of faith. Chapter 2 investigates how the coming of Christ redefined Israel, opening God's covenant to all believers. Chapter 3 delves into the early church's understanding of the Church as the True Israel, while Chapter 4 traces this view through centuries of Christian theology. Finally, Chapter 5 analyzes the emergence of dispensationalism and its profound impact on modern Christianity, particularly among evangelicals. The book concludes with a call to return to the historic roots of the faith, embracing the Church's identity as the True Israel and rejecting the theological errors of dispensationalism.

Written for both scholars and lay readers, this book seeks to balance theological depth with clarity, offering a concise yet compelling case for the Church as the True Israel. By grounding our exploration in Scripture and history, we hope to inspire Christians to reclaim their biblical identity, foster unity in the body of Christ, and engage thoughtfully with the world around them. Let us begin this journey by asking: Who is Israel, and what does it mean to be God's covenant people today?

Virgil A. Walker

Chapter 1: The Identity of Israel in the Old Testament

The question of who or what constitutes "Israel" begins in the pages of the Old Testament, where the term first emerges as both a personal name and a collective identity. To understand the True Israel, as this book seeks to define it, we must first explore the multifaceted nature of Israel in the Hebrew Scriptures. Is Israel merely a nation, defined by its ethnic and geographic boundaries, or does it carry a deeper, spiritual significance tied to faith in God's covenant promises? This chapter examines the origins of Israel, the covenant relationship that shapes its identity, and the theological implications of Old Testament texts that suggest a broader, more inclusive understanding of God's people.

The Origin of "Israel"

The name "Israel" first appears in Genesis 32:28, when God renames Jacob, the grandson of Abraham, after his wrestling encounter with a divine figure: "Your name shall no longer be called Jacob, but Israel, for you have striven with God and with men, and have prevailed." The Hebrew root *sarah* ("to strive" or "contend") imbues the name with a dynamic sense of persistence in faith, suggesting not merely a struggle but a transformative encounter with God that reshapes identity. This is reinforced in Hosea 12:3-4, where Jacob's wrestling is tied to his prophetic intercession, portraying Israel as one who prevails through reliance on God. From its inception, the term "Israel" is thus personal and relational, rooted in an individual's faith-filled engagement with the divine.

As the narrative of Genesis unfolds, Israel expands from a person to a people. The twelve sons of Jacob become the progenitors of the twelve tribes, and by the time of the Exodus, "Israel" refers to a collective—a community bound by shared ancestry and divine calling. In Exodus 1:7, the Israelites are described as a burgeoning people in Egypt, setting the stage for their liberation and formation as a nation. Yet, even in these early texts, Israel's identity is not solely ethnic or national but is deeply tied to God's covenant, a theme that recurs throughout the Old Testament.

Historical and Archaeological Contexts of Israel's Emergence

The biblical portrayal of Israel's origins as a people descending from Jacob is complemented by historical and archaeological perspectives that illuminate its early development. Scholars propose that Israel emerged as a distinct group in the Late Bronze Age (c. 1300–1200 BCE), possibly as a coalition of migrant slaves and pastoral nomads who escaped Egyptian oppression, as depicted in the Exodus narrative. The Merneptah Stele (c. 1208 BCE), an Egyptian inscription discovered by Flinders Petrie in 1896, provides the earliest extra-biblical reference to "Israel," describing it as a people group in Canaan: "Israel is wasted, bare of seed." This suggests a recognizable ethnic or social entity by this time, significant enough to merit mention alongside city-states like Ashkelon and Gezer. As Michael G. Hasel notes, "The stele's reference to Israel as a people, rather than a city or land, indicates a socioethnic group with a distinct identity in the late 13th century BCE."

This aligns with the biblical account of Israel's settlement in Canaan under Joshua, though archaeological evidence complicates the conquest narrative. Israel Finkelstein, a leading archaeologist, argues that the emergence of hundreds of small agricultural villages in the central hill country during the early Iron Age (c. 1200–1100 BCE) marks the formation of Israelite identity, likely through a gradual process of social integration rather than widespread military conquest. He writes, "The data for assigning the beginning of Israelite settlement to the 13th century are few and inconclusive," suggesting a 12th-century emergence for these settlements. This gradualist model contrasts with the biblical depiction but supports the presence of a group identified as "Israel" by the late 13th century, as evidenced by the Merneptah Stele.

Significantly, the "mixed multitude" mentioned in Exodus 12:38, which joined the Israelites in their exodus from Egypt, underscores that Israel's formation included non-ethnic elements from the outset. This diverse group, likely comprising other oppressed peoples or those drawn to

Israel's God, foreshadows the inclusive nature of God's covenant community. William G. Dever emphasizes this point, stating, "The Merneptah Stele's mention of Israel… suggests a group prominent enough to be perceived as a challenge to Egyptian hegemony, possibly including diverse elements united by a shared religious or social identity." These early hints of inclusivity challenge a strictly ethnic definition of Israel, suggesting that even at its origin, the community was shaped by a shared commitment to Yahweh's deliverance and promises. This blend of biblical narrative and historical context sets the stage for understanding Israel as a people defined by both divine calling and dynamic social formation, preparing the way for its evolving identity in the covenant relationship.

The Covenant Relationship

At the heart of Israel's identity lies its covenant relationship with God, which begins with Abraham and is reaffirmed through Moses. In Genesis 12:1-3, God calls Abraham, promising to make him "a great nation" and a blessing to "all the families of the earth." This Abrahamic covenant establishes Israel as a people chosen for a purpose: to reflect God's glory and mediate His blessing to the world. The covenant is not merely a contract but a relational bond, requiring faith and obedience, as seen in Abraham's trust in God's promises (Genesis 15:6).

The Mosaic covenant, formalized at Sinai, further shapes Israel's identity. In Exodus 19:5-6, God declares, "If you will indeed obey my voice and keep my covenant, you shall be my treasured possession among all peoples, for all the earth is mine; and you shall be to me a kingdom of priests and a holy nation." Here, Israel is defined not only by its national existence but by its calling to be a holy, priestly community, set apart to represent God to the nations. This passage introduces a tension: Israel is a nation with geographic and ethnic dimensions, yet its identity is inseparable from its spiritual role, which requires faithfulness to God.

The covenant relationship underscores that Israel's status as God's people is contingent on faith and obedience, not merely lineage. This is evident in moments of rebellion, such as the golden calf incident (Exodus 32), where God's judgment on unfaithfulness highlights that membership in Israel is not guaranteed by ethnicity alone. The Old Testament repeatedly emphasizes that true belonging to Israel involves a heart aligned with God's covenant (e.g., Deuteronomy 10:16, "Circumcise therefore the foreskin of your heart").

Covenantal Imagery and Typological Foundations

The covenantal identity of Israel is further enriched by the Davidic covenant and typological connections to God's broader redemptive plan. In 2 Samuel 7:12-16, God promises David an everlasting dynasty, declaring, "I will establish the throne of his kingdom forever." This covenant extends Israel's calling as a "kingdom of priests" (Exodus 19:6) to include a royal dimension, with the

Who is Israel?: A Historic Reflection of Church History

Davidic king mediating God's blessings to the nations and prefiguring a messianic hope. As G.K. Beale notes, "The Davidic covenant builds on earlier promises, positioning Israel as a conduit for God's rule over creation, fulfilled ultimately in Christ."

Typologically, Israel's covenant role echoes Adam's original mandate. As God's "son" (Exodus 4:22), Israel recapitulates Adam's roles as priest, prophet, and king (Genesis 2:15, 19-20), tasked with stewarding God's creation and reflecting His image corporately. Ezekiel 36:26-27 reinforces this, promising a new heart and spirit to enable covenant fidelity, undoing the curse of Adam's failure through a transformed people. John Goldingay observes, "Israel's election as God's son recalls Adam's role, suggesting a corporate vocation to restore creation through covenant obedience."

Covenantal imagery further deepens this identity. In Hosea 2:19-20, God portrays Israel as His "wife," betrothed in righteousness and steadfast love, emphasizing relational intimacy over mere legal obligation. Similarly, Psalm 80:8-11 depicts Israel as a "vine" transplanted from Egypt, intended to bear fruit for God's glory but subject to judgment for unfaithfulness. These images highlight that Israel's identity is dynamic, rooted in a living relationship with Yahweh that demands heart-level transformation. Jeremiah 31:31-34 anticipates a new covenant, internalizing this relationship through a law written on the heart, setting the stage for the New

Testament's fulfillment in Christ. Together, these elements portray Israel as a people called to embody God's redemptive purposes, transcending ethnicity through a faith-filled covenant bond that foreshadows the inclusive community of the Church.

Israel: Nation or People of Faith?

The question of whether Israel is primarily a nation or a spiritual community of faith runs through the Old Testament. On one hand, Israel is undeniably a nation, with a land (Canaan), a law (the Torah), and a distinct ethnic identity as the descendants of Abraham, Isaac, and Jacob. The conquest of Canaan under Joshua and the establishment of the monarchy under Saul, David, and Solomon solidify Israel's national identity, complete with political structures and territorial boundaries.

Yet, the Old Testament also hints at a broader, more inclusive understanding of Israel, one defined by faith rather than ethnicity. For example, non-Israelites like Rahab (Joshua 2) and Ruth (Ruth 1:16) are incorporated into God's people through their faith and allegiance to Israel's God. These stories suggest that God's covenant community transcends strict ethnic boundaries, embracing those who align with His purposes. The prophet Isaiah explicitly envisions this inclusivity, declaring that foreigners who join themselves to the Lord will be accepted as part of His people: "Their burnt offerings and their sacrifices will be accepted on my altar; for my house shall be called a house of prayer for all peoples" (Isaiah 56:6-8).

This tension between national and spiritual identity becomes even more pronounced in the prophetic literature. The prophets frequently critique Israel for its unfaithfulness, warning that God's judgment will fall on those who fail to live as His covenant people (e.g., Amos 5:21-24, Jeremiah 7:3-7). At the same time, they foretell a future restoration where God will gather a faithful remnant, not only from Israel but from all nations (e.g., Zechariah 8:20-23). These passages point to a vision of Israel that is not limited to a single nation but encompasses a universal community united by faith in God.

Postexilic Identity and the Remnant

The postexilic period further clarifies Israel's identity as a community defined by faith and covenant fidelity. After the Babylonian exile, the returnees under Ezra and Nehemiah rebuilt their identity around Torah observance and temple worship, as seen in Nehemiah 8, where the public reading of the Law unites the community. This era saw the rise of synagogue life, which fostered a shared commitment to God's Word and attracted "God-fearers"—Gentiles who embraced Israel's faith without full ethnic assimilation. William G. Dever observes, "Postexilic Israel's cohesion around Torah and temple suggests a shift toward a religious identity that could include sympathetic outsiders." This openness laid groundwork for the Second Temple period's broader inclusivity.

The prophetic concept of the "remnant" further refines this identity. Isaiah 10:20-22 describes a "remnant of Israel" that survives judgment by relying on God, not human strength, while Amos 9:8-15 promises restoration for a faithful subset who embody God's covenant. G.K. Beale notes, "The remnant motif underscores that true Israel is defined by faith, not merely ethnicity, anticipating the New Testament's inclusive community." This remnant vision, coupled with prophetic calls for universal inclusion (e.g., Isaiah 19:24-25, where Egypt and Assyria are called "my people"), foreshadows the Church as a fulfillment of Israel's calling. These developments highlight that, even within the Old Testament, Israel's identity evolves toward a faith-based community, transcending ethnic and geographic limits to embrace all who trust in Yahweh.

Theological Implications

The Old Testament's portrayal of Israel lays a critical foundation for the arguments of this book. While Israel begins as a specific people with a national identity, its deeper calling as a "kingdom of priests" and a "holy nation" suggests a spiritual dimension that transcends ethnicity and geography. The inclusion of faithful Gentiles and the emphasis on covenant obedience indicate that God's people are ultimately defined by their relationship with Him, not merely by birth or borders.

This understanding challenges any narrow view of Israel as solely a secular or ethnic entity. Even in the Old Testament, the seeds of a broader, faith-based identity are sown, preparing the way for the New Testament's continuation of Israel through Christ. As we will see in subsequent chapters, the coming of Jesus fulfills and expands the covenant, identifying the Church as the True Israel—a community of believers, Jew and Gentile, united by faith.

Israel in Ancient Near Eastern Context

Israel's covenantal identity stands in stark contrast to the national identities of its ancient Near Eastern neighbors. In Mesopotamian and Egyptian societies, identity was often tied to polytheistic worship and loyalty to a divine king, with gods like Marduk or Amun legitimizing political power. Israel, however, was defined by its monotheistic covenant with Yahweh, emphasizing ethical demands like justice and Sabbath observance (Deuteronomy 4:5-8). As John Goldingay notes, "Israel's identity was rooted in a unique relationship with one God, whose ethical requirements distinguished His people from surrounding nations." This covenantal framework made Israel a "holy nation" tasked with reflecting God's character to the world, rather than merely serving a ruler's agenda.

Scholars like Israel Finkelstein suggest the "twelve tribes" narrative may reflect a Judahite construct to unify diverse groups under a shared ancestry, particularly after the northern kingdom's fall (722 BCE). Finkelstein argues,

"The idea of a united Israel... was likely a Judahite ideological creation to assert hegemony over tribal memories." Yet, this "myth" served a theological purpose, fostering a collective identity centered on Yahweh's covenant, transcending historical divisions between Israel and Judah.

This inclusive vision finds its ultimate expression in passages like Isaiah 19:24-25, where God calls Egypt and Assyria "my people" alongside Israel, anticipating a universal covenant community. This foreshadows the Church, which fulfills Abraham's call to bless "all the families of the earth" (Genesis 12:3) by uniting Jew and Gentile in faith. As G.K. Beale observes, "The Old Testament's inclusive hints point to a continuation of Israel, fulfilled in Christ's body, the Church." Thus, the Old Testament's portrayal of Israel as a faith-based community sets the stage for its expansion into a global people of God, as explored in subsequent chapters.

Conclusion

The Old Testament presents Israel as both a nation and a people of faith, bound by God's covenant and called to reflect His holiness to the world. While its national identity is undeniable, the inclusion of faithful outsiders and the emphasis on covenant fidelity point to a spiritual identity that transcends physical boundaries. This multifaceted portrait of Israel sets the stage for the transformative work of Christ, who fulfilled the promises to God's people in a way that fulfills the Old Testament's promises and opens the covenant to all who believe. In the next chapter, we will explore how Jesus' life, death, and resurrection reshaped the identity of Israel, paving the way for the Church to emerge as the True Israel.

Sources:

Beale, G.K. *A New Testament Biblical Theology: The Unfolding of the Old Testament in the New*. Grand Rapids: Baker Academic, 2011

Goldingay, John. *Old Testament Theology: Israel's Gospel*. Downers Grove: InterVarsity Press, 2003

Finkelstein, Israel, and Neil Asher Silberman. *The Bible Unearthed: Archaeology's New Vision of Ancient Israel and the Origin of Its Sacred Texts*. New York: Free Press, 2001

Dever, William G. *Who Were the Early Israelites and Where Did They Come From?* Grand Rapids: Eerdmans, 2003

Hasel, Michael G. "Israel in the Merneptah Stele." *Bulletin of the American Schools of Oriental Research* 296 (1994): 45–61

Younger, K. Lawson, Jr. *Ancient Conquest Accounts: A Study in Ancient Near Eastern and Biblical History Writing*. Sheffield: JSOT Press, 1990

Ben-Tor, Amnon, ed. *The Archaeology of Ancient Israel*. New Haven: Yale University Press, 1992

Virgil A. Walker

Chapter 2: The Coming of Christ and the Continuation of Israel

The coming of Jesus Christ marks a pivotal moment in the biblical narrative, fundamentally reshaping the identity of Israel. In the Old Testament, as explored in Chapter 1, Israel was both a nation and a covenant community, defined by its relationship with God through faith and obedience. With the arrival of Christ, the New Testament reinterprets this identity, presenting Jesus as the fulfillment of God's promises and the one through whom the covenant is extended to all humanity. This chapter examines how Jesus' life, death, and resurrection redefined Israel, transforming it into a universal community of believers—the Church to go out to all nations across the world. By exploring key New Testament teachings, we will see that faith in Christ, not ethnicity or geography, becomes the defining mark of God's people, laying the foundation for the Church as the True Israel.

Jesus as the Fulfillment of the Law and Prophets

Central to the New Testament's fulfillment and continuation of Israel is the claim that Jesus fulfills the Law and the Prophets, embodying the promises made to

Israel in the Old Testament. In Matthew 5:17, Jesus declares, "Do not think that I have come to abolish the Law or the Prophets; I have not come to abolish them but to fulfill them." This statement positions Jesus as the culmination of God's covenant with Israel, the one through whom the promises to Abraham, Moses, and the prophets are realized. As the true seed of Abraham (Galatians 3:16), Jesus embodies the covenant's purpose: to bless all nations (Genesis 12:3).

Jesus' life and ministry demonstrate this fulfillment. His teachings, miracles, and obedience to God's will reveal Him as the perfect Israelite, embodying the faithfulness that the nation of Israel often lacked. For example, in the temptation narrative (Matthew 4:1-11), Jesus succeeds where Israel failed in the wilderness, resisting temptation and remaining faithful to God. Similarly, His role as the suffering servant (Isaiah 53) fulfills the prophetic vision of a figure who bears the sins of God's people, accomplishing redemption not only for Israel but for the world.

The Inclusion of the Gentiles

One of the most significant shifts in the New Testament is the inclusion of Gentiles in God's covenant, redefining Israel as a global universal community. The Old Testament hinted at this inclusivity (e.g., Isaiah 56:6-8), but Jesus' ministry makes it explicit. In John 4:21-24, Jesus tells the Samaritan woman that true worship is no longer tied to a specific place (Jerusalem or Samaria) but is defined by spirit and truth, opening the door for all people to worship God. His Great Commission (Matthew 28:19-20) commands the disciples to make disciples of *all nations*, signaling that the covenant promises are no longer restricted to ethnic Israel.

The apostle Paul articulates this fulfillment and continuation most clearly. In Romans 11:17-24, he uses the metaphor of an olive tree to describe how Gentile believers are grafted into Israel, sharing in the "root" of God's covenant promises. Similarly, in Galatians 3:28-29, Paul writes, "There is neither Jew nor Greek, slave nor free, male nor female, for you are all one in Christ Jesus. And if you are Christ's, then you are Abraham's offspring, heirs according to the promise." Here, Paul identifies believers in Christ—regardless of ethnicity—as the true heirs of Abraham, Israel as a spiritual community united by faith.

The New Israel in Christ

The New Testament presents the Church as the "new Israel," a community where faith in Christ, not ethnicity or adherence to the Mosaic Law, defines membership. This is evident in passages like Ephesians 2:11-22, where Paul describes how Christ's death has broken down the "dividing wall of hostility" between Jews and Gentiles, creating "one new man" in Himself. Through His sacrifice, Jesus establishes a new covenant (Luke 22:20), fulfilling and superseding the Mosaic covenant. The Church, as the body of Christ, becomes the locus of

God's covenant people, inheriting the promises made to Israel.

This is not a rejection of Israel's heritage but a fulfillment of its spiritual purpose. The New Testament writers consistently use Old Testament language to describe the Church, calling believers a "chosen race, a royal priesthood, a holy nation" (1 Peter 2:9), echoing Exodus 19:5-6. By applying these titles to the Church, the apostles affirm that God's plan has always been to create a people defined by faith, not merely by national identity.

Early Jewish-Christian Dynamics and the Identity of Israel

The transition from a Jewish-centered covenant community to a universal Church was complex, particularly in the first century. Early Jewish Christians, such as those in Jerusalem, initially maintained strong ties to the temple and Mosaic Law (Acts 21:20-24), viewing themselves as the faithful remnant of Israel. However, as Gentiles joined the Church in increasing numbers, tensions arose over issues like circumcision and dietary laws. The Epistle to the Hebrews addresses Jewish Christians hesitant to fully embrace the new covenant, arguing that Christ's priesthood and sacrifice surpass the old system (Hebrews 7:23-28, 10:11-14). The author presents Jesus as the mediator of a "better covenant" (Hebrews 8:6), fulfilling the promise of Jeremiah 31:31-34 for a law written on the heart.

Meanwhile, Jewish rejection of Jesus as Messiah led to a growing distinction between synagogue and Church. By the late first century, the Birkat HaMinim, a Jewish synagogue prayer cursing "heretics" (often interpreted as including Christians), signaled a formal separation. Yet, early Christian writers like Justin Martyr (c. 100–165 CE) argued that the Church was the "true Israel," inheriting the promises through faith in Christ (*Dialogue with Trypho*, 135). This perspective built on Paul's theology, emphasizing continuity with Israel's covenant while embracing its universal scope.

Addressing Objections to the Church as True Israel

The idea of the Church as the True Israel has faced objections, particularly from those who argue that it diminishes God's promises to ethnic Israel. Critics of "replacement theology" (or supersessionism) contend that God's covenant with Israel remains distinct and unfulfilled apart from a national restoration. However, the New Testament's view is better understood as *fulfillment theology*, not replacement. As G.K. Beale explains, "The Church does not replace Israel but expands it, incorporating all who share Abraham's faith into the covenant community" (*A New Testament Biblical Theology*, 2011). Romans 11:25-29 affirms God's ongoing commitment to Israel, suggesting that ethnic Jews remain part of God's plan, with their inclusion possible through faith in Christ.

Another objection is that equating the Church with Israel ignores the cultural and historical distinctiveness of the Jewish people. Yet, the New Testament emphasizes continuity, not erasure. The Church inherits Israel's spiritual calling while preserving the unique role of ethnic Jews within God's redemptive plan (Romans 3:1-2). The inclusion of Gentiles does not negate Israel's heritage but fulfills its purpose as a "light to the nations" (Isaiah 42:6).

Theological Implications

The fulfillment and continuation of Israel in the New Testament has profound implications for Christian theology. By fulfilling the Law and Prophets, Jesus becomes the focal point of God's covenant, making faith in Him the criterion for belonging to Israel. The inclusion of Gentiles dismantles ethnic and geographic barriers, creating a universal community that transcends the boundaries of the Old Testament nation. This shift does not negate God's promises to Israel but fulfills them in a way that expands their scope, inviting all people into the covenant through Christ.

This understanding challenges any view that limits Israel to a secular or ethnic entity. The New Testament presents the Church as the True Israel, not as a replacement for the Jewish people but as the continuation of God's covenant community, now open to all who believe. As we will explore in the next chapter, the early church embraced this vision, articulating the Church's identity as the heir of God's promises to Israel.

Conclusion

The coming of Christ marks a transformative moment in the identity of Israel, shifting it from a national entity to a worldwide universal community of faith. Through His fulfillment of the Law and Prophets, Jesus redefines God's people, making faith in Him the defining characteristic of the True Israel. The inclusion of Gentiles and the establishment of the Church as the new covenant community fulfill the Old Testament's vision of a people set apart for God. In the next chapter, we will examine how the early church fathers and apostolic teachings built on this foundation, solidifying the Church's identity as the True Israel in the first centuries of Christianity.

Sources:

- Beale, G.K. *A New Testament Biblical Theology: The Unfolding of the Old Testament in the New*. Grand Rapids: Baker Academic, 2011.

- Dunn, James D.G. *The Theology of Paul the Apostle*. Grand Rapids: Eerdmans, 1998.

- Hays, Richard B. *Echoes of Scripture in the Letters of Paul*. New Haven: Yale University Press, 1989.

- Wright, N.T. *Jesus and the Victory of God*. Minneapolis: Fortress Press, 1996.

- Justin Martyr. *Dialogue with Trypho*. Translated by Thomas B. Falls. Washington, DC: Catholic University of America Press, 2003.

Virgil A. Walker

Chapter 3: The Early Church Understanding of Israel

The New Testament's redefinition of Israel as a universal community of faith, centered on Jesus Christ, marked a pivotal shift in the biblical narrative, setting the stage for the early church's theological reflection on its identity as God's covenant people. As explored in Chapters 1 and 2, the Old Testament presents Israel as both a nation and a spiritual community, bound by God's covenant promises to Abraham, Moses, and David, with hints of an inclusive vision encompassing all nations (e.g., Isaiah 56:6-8). With the coming of Christ, the New Testament fulfilled these promises, transforming Israel's identity into a global community—the Church—united by faith rather than ethnicity or geography. This chapter examines how the apostles and early church fathers articulated this transformation, consistently identifying the Church as the True Israel, the heir of God's covenant through Christ's fulfillment of the Law and Prophets. By analyzing key apostolic teachings, particularly Paul's theology of the remnant and the olive tree (Romans 9–11), the robust exegesis of fathers like Justin Martyr, Irenaeus, Origen, and Augustine, and pivotal historical events like the destruction of the Jerusalem Temple in 70 CE, we will demonstrate the early church's unified vision of the Church as the culmination of Israel's spiritual calling.

Who is Israel?: A Historic Reflection of Church History

This vision was not a rejection of Israel's heritage but its organic continuation and expansion, fulfilling the Abrahamic promise to bless "all the families of the earth" (Genesis 12:3). The early church understood the Church as the "spiritual Israel," embodying the remnant theology of the prophets (e.g., Isaiah 10:20-22; Romans 11:5), where God's promises are realized through a faithful subset defined by allegiance to Christ. Typologically, Israel's institutions—such as the Temple, priesthood, and sacrifices—served as shadows pointing to Christ and His body, the Church, as their fulfillment (e.g., Hebrews 8:6; John 2:19-21). This perspective, often termed "economic supersessionism," reflects God's progressive economy of salvation, where the old covenant naturally transitions to the new, not as a replacement but as a completion that universalizes Israel's calling. Modern critiques frequently mischaracterize this as "replacement theology," accusing it of negating God's promises to ethnic Israel or fostering anti-Judaism. Such critiques overlook the early church's emphasis on continuity: the Church inherits Israel's spiritual mantle while preserving God's enduring faithfulness to His covenant, as Paul affirms, "The gifts and the calling of God are irrevocable" (Romans 11:29).

The early church navigated complex Jewish-Christian tensions, particularly after the Temple's destruction, which forced both Judaism and Christianity to redefine their identities. While Judaism reoriented around rabbinic traditions, Christians saw the Temple's fall as confirmation of Christ's prophecy (Matthew 24:1-2) and

His role as the new temple (John 2:19-21), shifting God's presence to the Church. Through typology, remnant theology, and the lens of covenant continuity, this chapter will trace how the apostles and fathers articulated the Church as the True Israel, a universal community open to all who believe. This theology not only countered challenges like Gnosticism and Judaizing tendencies but also laid a foundation for Christian identity that persisted through centuries, shaping the Church's mission as a "light to the nations" (Isaiah 42:6). By grounding their arguments in Scripture and historical context, early Christian thinkers affirmed that God's plan, from Abraham to Christ, was always to create a people defined by faith, fulfilling Israel's purpose on a global scale.

Apostolic Teachings and Paul's Theology

The apostles, particularly Paul, laid the foundational theology for the early church's understanding of Israel, articulating the Church as the heir of God's covenant promises through faith in Jesus Christ. Building on the New Testament's vision of Christ's fulfillment of the Law and Prophets (Chapter 2), Paul's epistles provide a robust framework for identifying the Church as the True Israel. In Romans 9–11, Paul grapples with the question of Israel's place in God's redemptive plan, asserting that the promises to Israel have not failed but are fulfilled through a remnant chosen by grace: "At the present time there is a remnant, chosen by grace" (Romans 11:5). This remnant, comprising both Jewish and Gentile believers, embodies the "Israel of God" (Galatians 6:16), a community defined not by ethnic descent but by faith in Christ. Paul's metaphor of the olive tree (Romans 11:17–24) vividly illustrates this continuity and expansion: Gentile believers are grafted into the covenantal root of Israel, sharing in its promises alongside faithful Jews, while unfaithful branches are broken off due to unbelief. As G.K. Beale notes, "Paul's imagery underscores that true Israel is defined by faith, not ethnicity, fulfilling the prophetic vision of a faithful remnant (Isaiah 10:20-22)."

Paul's theology is deeply typological, portraying Christ as the true Israel who fulfills the nation's calling. In Galatians 3:16, Paul identifies Christ as the singular "seed" of Abraham, through whom the promises of blessing to all nations (Genesis 12:3) are realized. Believers, united to Christ, become "Abraham's offspring, heirs according to the promise" (Galatians 3:29), transcending ethnic and social barriers: "There is neither Jew nor Greek, slave nor free, male nor female, for you are all one in Christ Jesus" (Galatians 3:28). This universal vision echoes the Old Testament's inclusive hints (e.g., Isaiah 56:6-8) and redefines Israel as a spiritual community centered on Christ's redemptive work. Paul's emphasis on the new covenant, promised in Jeremiah 31:31-34, further solidifies this shift. In 2 Corinthians 3:6-14, he contrasts the fading glory of the Mosaic covenant with the surpassing glory of the new covenant in Christ, where the Spirit writes God's law on believers' hearts, fulfilling Israel's spiritual purpose.

Virgil A. Walker

Other apostolic writings reinforce this understanding. The Epistle to the Hebrews presents Christ as the mediator of a "better covenant" (Hebrews 8:6), rendering the Mosaic covenant "obsolete" (Hebrews 8:13). The author argues that Christ's eternal priesthood and once-for-all sacrifice (Hebrews 7:23-28, 10:11-14) fulfill and surpass the Levitical system, making the Church—comprising all believers—the new covenant community. Typologically, Hebrews portrays Israel's institutions as shadows pointing to Christ: the Temple prefigures His body (John 2:19-21), and the Exodus through the Red Sea foreshadows baptism (1 Corinthians 10:1-4). Similarly, 1 Peter 2:9-10 applies Old Testament titles for Israel—"a chosen race, a royal priesthood, a holy nation" (Exodus 19:5-6)—to the Church, affirming its identity as God's people, "who once were not a people, but now are God's people." These texts collectively establish a foundational apostolic teaching: the Church is the True Israel, fulfilling the spiritual purpose of God's covenant through faith in Christ.

Early non-canonical apostolic writings further echo this theology. The Didache (c. 50-120 CE), an early Christian manual, applies Old Testament covenant ethics to the Church, instructing believers to live as a holy community in anticipation of Christ's return. Its use of the "Two Ways" teaching (Didache 1-6) draws on Deuteronomy's call to choose life (Deuteronomy 30:19), implying the Church's continuity with Israel's covenantal calling. Likewise, 1 Clement (c. 95 CE), attributed to Clement of

Who is Israel?: A Historic Reflection of Church History

Rome, urges the Corinthian church to emulate the harmony of Israel under Moses, applying Old Testament language to the Church as a unified people of God: "Let us be joined to those who practice peace with godliness" (1 Clement 15). This continuity is evident in Clement's use of Isaiah's remnant imagery, reinforcing the Church as the faithful subset of God's people.

This apostolic vision was not without challenges. Some Jewish Christians in the first century maintained adherence to the Mosaic Law (Acts 21:20-24), raising questions about the Church's relationship to ethnic Israel. Paul addresses this in Romans 9:6-8, asserting, "Not all who are descended from Israel belong to Israel," emphasizing that true membership is through faith, not physical descent. Critics of the "Church as True Israel" view often point to Romans 11:25-29, particularly the phrase "all Israel will be saved," to argue for a distinct future restoration of ethnic Israel apart from the Church. However, Paul's context suggests a broader interpretation: "all Israel" encompasses the full number of God's elect—Jew and Gentile—gathered through faith in Christ across history. As N.T. Wright argues, "Paul's vision in Romans 11 is not a separate plan for ethnic Israel but the culmination of God's promise to Abraham, fulfilled in a multi-ethnic community united in Christ." This aligns with the remnant theology of the prophets, where God preserves a faithful core (e.g., Amos 9:8-15) now realized in the Church.

The apostolic teachings, particularly Paul's, thus provide a theological cornerstone for the early church's understanding of Israel. By emphasizing faith in Christ as the criterion for covenant membership, employing typology to show Christ's fulfillment of Israel's roles (e.g., as true seed, priest, and temple), and envisioning a universal community, the apostles laid a robust foundation for the Church as the True Israel. This framework not only countered Judaizing tendencies but also set the stage for the early church fathers to articulate a cohesive ecclesiology, as explored in the following sections.

Early Church Fathers and the True Israel

The early church fathers, writing in the first few centuries, built on this apostolic foundation, consistently identifying the Church as the True Israel. Their writings, shaped by apologetic, pastoral, and theological concerns, provide robust evidence of this consensus. Justin Martyr, in his *Dialogue with Trypho* (c. 150 CE), argues that Christians are the "true Israel" because they fulfill the promises given to Abraham through faith in Christ. He interprets Old Testament prophecies, such as those in Isaiah, as pointing to the Church, which inherits the covenant through Jesus, the true seed of Abraham (Galatians 3:16). Justin's dialogue with Trypho, a Jewish interlocutor, reflects the early church's need to distinguish itself from Judaism while affirming its continuity with God's promises.

Who is Israel?: A Historic Reflection of Church History

Irenaeus of Lyons (c. 180 CE), in *Against Heresies*, further develops this theology. He emphasizes the unity of God's plan across the Old and New Testaments, arguing that the Church fulfills Israel's calling to be a light to the nations. For Irenaeus, Christ recapitulates Israel's history, succeeding where the nation failed, and the Church, as His body, inherits the covenant promises. His emphasis on the continuity of God's economy (plan of salvation) underscores the Church's identity as the True Israel.

Origen of Alexandria (c. 185–254 CE) offers a particularly rich contribution through his allegorical and typological approach to Scripture. In his *Homilies on Joshua* and *Commentary on the Song of Songs*, Origen interprets Old Testament narratives as prefiguring Christ and the Church. For example, he sees the Israelites' crossing of the Jordan River as a type of baptism, with the Church as the new Israel entering the promised land of salvation. Origen argues that the Old Testament's promises to Israel find their spiritual fulfillment in the Church, which embodies God's universal covenant community. His method of allegory, while sometimes controversial, was influential in reinforcing the Church's identity as the True Israel, as it allowed early Christians to see their faith as the culmination of God's plan.

Augustine of Hippo (c. 354–430 CE) provides one of the most comprehensive articulations of the Church as the True Israel. In his monumental *City of God*, Augustine traces the history of God's people from creation to eternity, arguing that the Church encompasses both Old Testament saints and New Testament believers. He views the Church as the "City of God," distinct from the earthly city, and identifies it as the heir of Israel's promises through Christ. In his *Tractates on the Gospel of John*, Augustine interprets passages like John 15 (the vine and branches) as evidence that the Church, united to Christ, is the true continuation of Israel, embracing all who share in faith. Augustine's theology also addresses Jewish-Christian relations, urging respect for the Jewish people as part of God's plan, even as he affirms the Church's role as the covenant community. His emphasis on the unity of salvation history solidified the early church's understanding of the Church as the True Israel.

Cyprian of Carthage (c. 250 CE), in his *Treatise on the Unity of the Church*, briefly reinforces this view, describing the Church as the new Israel united under Christ, the true high priest. His focus on ecclesial unity underscores the Church's universal nature, transcending ethnic and geographic boundaries. Together, these voices—spanning diverse regions, centuries, and theological approaches—demonstrate a consistent belief that the Church is the True Israel, fulfilling God's covenant promises.

Basil the Great (c. 330–379 CE), in *On the Holy Spirit* (Chapter 15), presents the Church as the eschatological community united by the Spirit, fulfilling Israel's call to be a "kingdom of priests" (Exodus 19:6). He argues that baptism incorporates all believers into God's covenant,

Who is Israel?: A Historic Reflection of Church History

echoing Isaiah's vision of a universal house of prayer (Isaiah 56:7). Gregory of Nazianzus (c. 329–390 CE), in his *Orations* (Oration 38 on the Theophany), poetically depicts the Church as the "new Jerusalem" (Galatians 4:26), where Christ's incarnation fulfills Israel's messianic hopes, uniting Jew and Gentile in faith. His lyrical style appeals to the heart, complementing Western systematic theology.

Gregory of Nazianzus and the Church as the New Jerusalem

Gregory of Nazianzus (c. 329–390 CE), known as the "Theologian" for his profound contributions to Trinitarian doctrine, played a pivotal role in articulating the Church's identity as the True Israel. As a Cappadocian Father alongside Basil the Great and Gregory of Nyssa, his lyrical and theological writings, particularly his *Theological Orations* (c. 379–381 CE) and *Oration 38 on the Theophany* (c. 381 CE), reinforced the early church's understanding of the Church as the fulfillment of Israel's covenant promises. Gregory's poetic and pastoral approach complemented the systematic exegesis of figures like Origen and Augustine, offering a vision of the Church as the "new Jerusalem" (Galatians 4:26), where Jew and Gentile are united in Christ's redemptive work.

In *Oration 38*, delivered on the feast of the Theophany (Christ's baptism), Gregory portrays the incarnation as the fulfillment of Israel's messianic hopes, transforming God's people into a universal community. He declares,

Virgil A. Walker

"Christ is born, the Law is fulfilled, and the nations are called to the light of the new Jerusalem" (*Oration 38.4*). By invoking the imagery of the "new Jerusalem" from Galatians 4:26 and Revelation 21:2, Gregory aligns the Church with the eschatological vision of Israel, where God's covenant embraces all who believe. His emphasis on Christ's incarnation as the pivotal moment in salvation history echoes Paul's theology in Romans 11:17–24, where Gentiles are grafted into Israel's covenantal root. For Gregory, the Church is not a replacement for Israel but its expansion, fulfilling the Abrahamic promise to bless all nations (Genesis 12:3).

Gregory's *Theological Orations*, delivered in Constantinople to counter Arianism, further underscore the Church's identity as the True Israel. In *Oration 31*, he defends the divinity of the Holy Spirit, arguing that the Spirit's work unites believers into one body, fulfilling Israel's call to be a "kingdom of priests" (Exodus 19:6). He writes, "Through the Spirit, we are made children of God, heirs of the promise, no longer strangers but citizens of the heavenly polity" (*Oration 31.29*). This language draws on Ephesians 2:19 and 1 Peter 2:9, applying Old Testament titles for Israel to the Church, which Gregory sees as the spiritual community united by faith in the Triune God. His Trinitarian theology grounds the Church's universality, as the Spirit's transformative power transcends ethnic and geographic boundaries, echoing Isaiah's vision of a "house of prayer for all peoples" (Isaiah 56:7).

Who is Israel?: A Historic Reflection of Church History

Gregory's contribution also lies in his pastoral emphasis on unity, a critical aspect of the Church's identity as the True Israel. In *Oration 6 on Peace*, he urges believers to overcome divisions, reflecting the Church's role as the reconciled community foretold in Zechariah 8:20–23. His lyrical style, blending theology with poetic imagery, made this vision accessible to both scholars and laypeople, reinforcing the Church's mission to reflect God's glory as a unified body. As N.T. Wright notes, "Gregory's theology of the Trinity and the Church's universal calling builds on Paul's vision of a multi-ethnic community, fulfilling Israel's purpose as a light to the nations" (*Paul and the Faithfulness of God*, 2013).

The Shift to Universal Ecclesiology

The early church's transition from a Jewish-centric movement to a universal ecclesiology marked a profound development in its understanding of itself as the True Israel. Rooted in Jesus' command to "make disciples of all nations" (Matthew 28:19-20) and enacted through pivotal events like the conversion of Cornelius (Acts 10), this shift fulfilled Old Testament prophecies of a covenant community embracing all peoples (e.g., Isaiah 56:6-8; Zechariah 8:20-23). The apostles and early church fathers articulated the Church as a global body, united by faith in Christ rather than ethnicity or adherence to the Mosaic Law. This section examines how key moments, such as the Council of Jerusalem, and early Christian writings, including the *Apostolic Constitutions*, reinforced this universal vision, establishing the Church as the fulfillment of Israel's calling to be a "light to the nations" (Isaiah 42:6).

The Council of Jerusalem (Acts 15, c. 49 CE) was a defining moment in this shift. As Gentile believers joined the Church in increasing numbers, tensions arose over whether they needed to follow Mosaic practices like circumcision. The apostles, led by Peter and James, affirmed that Gentiles were not required to become Jews to share in God's covenant, declaring, "We believe that we will be saved through the grace of the Lord Jesus, just as they will" (Acts 15:11). This decision, grounded in Amos 9:11-12 (quoted by James), interpreted the restoration of David's tent as the inclusion of Gentiles in God's people, fulfilling the prophetic vision of a universal covenant community. As N.T. Wright notes, "The Council of Jerusalem marked the Church's recognition that God's plan was always to extend Israel's privileges to all nations through faith in Christ." This ecclesiological shift redefined Israel not as a national entity but as a spiritual community open to all who believe.

New Testament writings further underscore this universality. In Acts 10, Peter's vision of the clean and unclean animals (Acts 10:9-16) and Cornelius' conversion signify that God "shows no partiality" (Acts 10:34), dismantling ethnic barriers. Paul's ministry to the Gentiles, described in Acts 13:46-48, fulfills Isaiah 49:6, where God's servant is a "light for the Gentiles" to bring salvation "to the ends of the earth." Ephesians 2:11-22 encapsulates this theology, portraying Christ's death as breaking down the "dividing wall of hostility" between Jew and Gentile, creating "one new man" in the Church. These texts collectively affirm that the Church, as the True Israel, inherits Israel's covenant promises through faith, transcending geographic and ethnic boundaries.

Early Christian writings outside the New Testament reinforce this universal ecclesiology. The *Apostolic Constitutions* (c. 380 CE), a compilation of earlier traditions, applies Old Testament covenant ethics to the Church, instructing bishops and believers to live as a holy community mirroring Israel's priestly calling (Exodus 19:6). For example, Book 2 emphasizes the Church's role as a unified body, drawing on Deuteronomy's communal laws to guide Christian conduct: "Let the bishop, as a high priest, minister to the people, uniting them as Israel was united under Moses" (*Apostolic Constitutions* 2.25). Similarly, Ignatius of Antioch (c. 35-108 CE) emphasizes ecclesial unity across cultures in his letters, urging believers to gather under one bishop as a reflection of the Church's universal nature: "Wherever the bishop is, there let the people be, just as wherever Jesus Christ is, there is the catholic Church" (*Letter to the Smyrnaeans* 8.2). These writings echo the apostolic vision, portraying the Church as the new Israel, fulfilling prophecies like Isaiah 56:6-8, where foreigners join God's people in worship.

This shift was not without challenges. Early Jewish Christians, particularly in Jerusalem, maintained strong ties to the Law (Acts 21:20-24), creating tensions with Gentile believers. The rise of Judaizing movements, which insisted on circumcision for salvation, prompted Paul's sharp rebuke in Galatians 5:2-4, affirming that faith in Christ, not ritual observance, defines God's people. The *Didache* (c. 50-120 CE) also navigates these tensions, applying Israel's ethical framework to a mixed Jewish-Gentile community while emphasizing baptism and the Eucharist as new covenant practices (*Didache* 7-9). By the second century, the Church's universal ecclesiology was firmly established, with fathers like Justin Martyr arguing that the Church's inclusion of Gentiles fulfills Israel's purpose as a "house of prayer for all peoples" (Isaiah 56:7; *Dialogue with Trypho* 116).

Theologically, this universal ecclesiology underscores the continuity of God's covenant. The Church inherits Israel's role as a "kingdom of priests" (Exodus 19:6; 1 Peter 2:9), mediating God's blessing to the world through faith in Christ. This fulfills the Abrahamic covenant's promise to bless all nations (Genesis 12:3) and the prophetic remnant motif, where a faithful subset—now Jew and Gentile—carries forward God's plan (Romans 11:5). Critics may argue that this shift marginalizes ethnic Israel, but the apostolic vision, as articulated by Paul, affirms God's ongoing faithfulness: "The gifts and the calling of God are irrevocable" (Romans 11:29). The Church does not replace Israel but expands it, incorporating all who share Abraham's faith into the covenant community.

This universal ecclesiology shaped the early church's identity and mission, setting the stage for the patristic articulation of the Church as the True Israel. The Council of Jerusalem, New Testament teachings, and early writings like the *Apostolic Constitutions* collectively demonstrate that God's plan was always to create a people defined by faith, fulfilling Israel's spiritual calling on a global scale. This foundation influenced subsequent theological developments, as explored in the following sections.

The Destruction of the Temple and Its Impact

The destruction of the Jerusalem Temple in 70 CE by Roman forces under Titus was a watershed moment that profoundly shaped the early church's understanding of its identity as the True Israel. For many Jews, the Temple was the heart of worship and national identity, symbolizing God's presence and covenant with Israel. Its loss raised existential questions about the continuation of God's promises, prompting both Judaism and Christianity to redefine their identities. Early Christians interpreted this event as a divine confirmation of Jesus' prophecy (Matthew 24:1-2) and His role as the new temple (John 2:19-21), signaling the transition from the old covenant to the new. The apostles and church fathers saw the Temple's destruction as evidence that God's presence now dwelt in the Church, the spiritual Israel, fulfilling the

Old Testament's prophetic vision of a universal covenant community (e.g., Isaiah 56:6-8). This section examines how this pivotal event, coupled with patristic exegesis, reinforced the Church's identity as the heir of Israel's covenant promises while navigating complex Jewish-Christian relations.

Jesus' prediction of the Temple's destruction—"not one stone will be left upon another" (Matthew 24:2)—set the stage for early Christian interpretation. In John 2:19-21, Jesus declares, "Destroy this temple, and in three days I will raise it up," referring to His body as the new locus of God's presence. The apostles understood this as a shift from a physical to a spiritual temple, fulfilled in Christ's resurrection and extended to the Church as His body (1 Corinthians 3:16-17; Ephesians 2:19-22). The author of Hebrews reinforces this, portraying Christ's sacrifice as surpassing the Temple's offerings, rendering the old system obsolete (Hebrews 10:11-14). The destruction of the physical Temple in 70 CE was thus seen as a divine ratification of this transition, confirming that God's covenant now operated through a universal community defined by faith, not a specific place or ritual.

Patristic writers built on this apostolic foundation, interpreting the Temple's destruction as a theological milestone. Justin Martyr, in his *Dialogue with Trypho* (c. 150 CE), argues that the Temple's fall fulfilled Old Testament prophecies of judgment for unfaithfulness (e.g., Jeremiah 7:13-14), while Christ's sacrifice established a new, spiritual worship: "The sacrifices of the priests are fulfilled in the offerings of the Church, which is the true Israel" (*Dialogue* 41). Tertullian, in *Adversus Judaeos* (c. 200 CE), sees the event as confirming the new covenant's supremacy: "The destruction of the Temple shows that God has rejected the old sacrifices, establishing Christ as the true altar" (*Adversus Judaeos* 13). Origen, in his *Homilies on Jeremiah*, interprets the Temple's fall allegorically as the end of the old covenant's shadows, with the Church as the new temple where God dwells: "The true temple is the heart of believers, united in Christ" (*Homilies on Jeremiah* 16.5). Eusebius of Caesarea (c. 260-340 CE), in his *Ecclesiastical History*, views the destruction as a divine judgment that paved the way for the Church's universal mission: "The ruin of Jerusalem opened the door for the gospel to all nations" (*Ecclesiastical History* 3.5). These interpretations collectively affirm the Church as the True Israel, inheriting Israel's spiritual role as a "kingdom of priests" (Exodus 19:6; 1 Peter 2:9).

Theologically, the Temple's destruction underscored both punitive and fulfillment elements of covenant theology. The punitive aspect, rooted in prophetic warnings (e.g., Micah 3:12), saw the event as judgment for Israel's unfaithfulness, aligning with the remnant theology of Romans 11:5, where a faithful subset—now the Church—carries forward God's plan. The fulfillment aspect, emphasized by the fathers, highlighted Christ as the true temple and sacrifice, fulfilling the Old Testament's types (e.g., the Passover lamb in Exodus 12; cf. 1 Corinthians

5:7). As G.K. Beale notes, "The Temple's destruction confirmed the apostolic teaching that Christ and His Church are the new sanctuary, fulfilling Israel's purpose to mediate God's presence to the world." This shift fulfilled prophecies like Isaiah 19:24-25, where God's people include Gentiles, reflecting the Abrahamic covenant's universal scope (Genesis 12:3).

The destruction also reshaped Jewish-Christian relations. As Judaism reoriented around rabbinic traditions and synagogue worship, Christians increasingly distinguished their identity, with events like the *Birkat HaMinim* (c. 90 CE), a synagogue prayer cursing "heretics," marking a formal separation. Some patristic rhetoric, such as Tertullian's, could be sharp, reflecting tensions post-70 CE. However, figures like Augustine balanced this by advocating respect for Jews as "witnesses" to Scripture, preserving their role in salvation history (*City of God* 18.46). Critics may argue that early Christian interpretations of the Temple's fall fueled anti-Judaism, but the fathers' focus was theological fulfillment, not ethnic rejection. The Church was seen as expanding Israel's covenant to include all nations, not negating God's promises, which remain "irrevocable" (Romans 11:29).

The destruction of the Temple thus solidified the early church's ecclesiology, affirming the Church as the True Israel. By interpreting the event through New Testament prophecies and typological exegesis, the fathers reinforced the continuity of God's covenant while embracing its universal expansion. This theological shift, grounded in Christ's fulfillment of Israel's roles, shaped the Church's identity and mission, as explored in subsequent sections.

Theological Implications

The early church's identification of the Church as the True Israel affirmed the continuity of God's covenant across the Old and New Testaments, with Christ as the fulfillment of Israel's promises. The expanded testimony of Origen and Augustine, with their allegorical and historical approaches, underscores the depth of this consensus. The Church was seen as a universal community, open to all who believe, challenging any notion that Israel's identity remained tied to a specific nation or land.

Critics of this view, particularly those advocating for a distinct future restoration of ethnic Israel, often label it "replacement theology," arguing it diminishes God's promises to the Jewish people. However, the early church's perspective is better understood as fulfillment theology, not replacement. Paul's assertion that "the gifts and the calling of God are irrevocable" (Romans 11:29) underscores God's ongoing commitment to ethnic Israel, with their inclusion possible through faith in Christ (Romans 11:23-24). The Church expands Israel's covenant, incorporating Gentiles as co-heirs without negating the Jewish people's unique role as bearers of God's oracles (Romans 3:1-2). Augustine's call to respect Jews as "witnesses" to Scripture (*City of God* 18.46) further balances this theology, countering accusations of anti-Judaism by affirming the Jewish people's place in salvation history. As R. Kendall Soulen notes, "Economic supersessionism sees the old covenant as preparatory, fulfilled in the new without annulling God's faithfulness to Israel." This framework challenges any notion that Israel's identity remains tied to a specific nation or land, instead presenting the Church as the universal community embodying God's redemptive purposes.

The theological implications extend to the Church's mission and identity. By inheriting Israel's roles as a priestly nation and light to the world, the Church is called to reflect God's holiness and mediate His blessing to all nations, fulfilling the Abrahamic covenant (Genesis 12:3). This universal scope dismantles ethnic and geographic barriers, affirming that faith in Christ is the sole criterion for membership in God's people. The early church's theology thus provides a robust foundation for Christian identity, rooted in the continuity of God's covenant and its expansion through Christ's redemptive work.

Conclusion

The early church, through apostolic teachings and the robust exegesis of the church fathers, consistently identified the Church as the True Israel, inheriting the covenant promises through faith in Jesus Christ. From Paul's theology of the remnant and the olive tree (Romans 9–11) to the typological interpretations of Origen, Irenaeus, and Justin Martyr, early Christians articulated a

Who is Israel?: A Historic Reflection of Church History

vision of the Church as the fulfillment of Israel's spiritual calling. The shift to a universal ecclesiology, catalyzed by events like the Council of Jerusalem and the destruction of the Temple in 70 CE, solidified this understanding, affirming that God's plan was always to create a people defined by faith, not ethnicity. Patristic writings, such as Augustine's *City of God* and Tertullian's *Adversus Judaeos*, reinforced this through typology and covenant continuity, portraying the Church as the new temple and priestly nation mediating God's blessing to all peoples.

This theology was not a rejection of Israel's heritage but its expansion, fulfilling the Abrahamic promise to bless all nations (Genesis 12:3) and the prophetic vision of a remnant faithful to God (Isaiah 10:20-22). The early church navigated challenges, such as Jewish-Christian tensions and Judaizing movements, by emphasizing the new covenant's supremacy (Hebrews 8:6) and the Church's universal mission (Matthew 28:19-20). Far from diminishing God's promises, this perspective upholds their irrevocability (Romans 11:29), inviting all—Jew and Gentile—into the covenant through faith. In the next chapter, we will explore how this theology persisted through medieval and Reformation thought, shaping the Church's identity until the emergence of modern interpretations that grapple with Israel's role in God's plan.

Sources:

- Beale, G.K. *A New Testament Biblical Theology: The Unfolding of the Old Testament in the New.* Grand Rapids: Baker Academic, 2011.

- Holmes, Michael W. *The Apostolic Fathers: Greek Texts and English Translations.* Grand Rapids: Baker Academic, 2007.

- Soulen, R. Kendall. *The God of Israel and Christian Theology.* Minneapolis: Fortress Press, 1996.

- Wright, N.T. *Paul and the Faithfulness of God.* Minneapolis: Fortress Press, 2013.

- Justin Martyr. *Dialogue with Trypho.* Translated by Thomas B. Falls. Washington, DC: Catholic University of America Press, 2003.

- Augustine. *City of God.* Translated by Henry Bettenson. London: Penguin Classics, 2003.

- *Apostolic Constitutions.* In *Ante-Nicene Fathers*, vol. 7, edited by Alexander Roberts and James Donaldson. Peabody: Hendrickson Publishers, 1994.

- Tertullian. *Adversus Judaeos.* In *Ante-Nicene Fathers*, vol. 3, edited by Alexander Roberts and James Donaldson. Peabody: Hendrickson Publishers, 1994.

- Origen. *Homilies on Jeremiah.* In *The Fathers of the Church*, vol. 97, translated by John Clark Smith.

Washington, DC: Catholic University of America Press, 1998.

- Eusebius. *Ecclesiastical History*. Translated by Kirsopp Lake. Cambridge: Harvard University Press, 1926.

- Irenaeus. *Against Heresies*. In *Ante-Nicene Fathers*, vol. 1, edited by Alexander Roberts and James Donaldson. Peabody: Hendrickson Publishers, 1994.

- Basil the Great. *On the Holy Spirit*. Translated by Stephen Hildebrand. Crestwood: St. Vladimir's Seminary Press, 2011.

Virgil A. Walker

Chapter 4: The Historic Church as Israel

The early church's identification of the Church as the True Israel, as explored in Chapter 3, became a cornerstone of Christian theology, shaping the Church's self-understanding for centuries. From the apostolic era through the medieval period and into the Reformation, theologians consistently affirmed that the Church, as the body of Christ, inherited the covenant promises made to Israel in the Old Testament. This chapter traces the persistence of this theology across church history, examining key figures like Augustine, medieval scholars, and Reformers such as Martin Luther and John Calvin, who reinforced the Church's identity as the True Israel. We will also explore the role of typology and allegory in interpreting Old Testament promises, address challenges to this view, and highlight its dominance until the 19th century, setting the stage for the radical shift introduced by dispensationalism.

Augustine and the Patristic Legacy

The theology of the Church as the True Israel was firmly established by Augustine of Hippo (354–430 CE), whose influence reverberated through subsequent centuries. In his *City of God*, Augustine presents the Church as the eternal community of God's people, encompassing both

Old Testament saints and New Testament believers. He argues that the promises made to Israel—such as the land, the kingdom, and the priesthood—find their ultimate fulfillment in Christ and His Church. For Augustine, the Church is the "City of God," distinct from earthly kingdoms, and its members are the true heirs of Abraham through faith (Galatians 3:29). His *Tractates on the Gospel of John* further develop this idea, portraying the Church as the spiritual Israel, united to Christ as branches to the vine (John 15:1–5).

Augustine's theology was not isolated but built on the patristic consensus of earlier fathers like Justin Martyr and Origen (Chapter 3). His comprehensive view of salvation history provided a framework for later theologians, ensuring that the identification of the Church as Israel remained a central tenet of Christian thought. Augustine also addressed Jewish-Christian relations, advocating respect for the Jewish people while affirming the Church's role as the covenant community, a balanced approach that influenced medieval theology.

Medieval Theology and the Church as Israel

Throughout the medieval period (roughly 500–1500 CE), the Church's identity as the True Israel remained a dominant theological theme. Theologians like Thomas Aquinas (1225–1274) reinforced this view, using scholastic methods to articulate the continuity of God's covenant. In his *Summa Theologica*, Aquinas argues that the Old Testament Law was a preparation for Christ, who fulfilled its promises, making the Church the spiritual heir of Israel. Medieval liturgy and art further reflected this theology, with Old Testament figures like Moses and David depicted as types of Christ, and the Church portrayed as the new Jerusalem.

The use of typology and allegory was central to medieval exegesis. Theologians interpreted Old Testament events and promises as prefiguring the Church. For example, the Exodus was seen as a type of Christ's redemption, with the Church as the new Israel delivered from the bondage of sin. The Song of Songs was allegorized as a love story between Christ and His Church, reinforcing the covenant relationship. This interpretive approach, rooted in the patristic tradition, allowed the Church to claim the spiritual promises of Israel while acknowledging their historical context.

Key Medieval Theologians and Their Contributions

As scholasticism emerged, Anselm of Canterbury (1033–1109 CE) contributed to this framework through his emphasis on satisfaction theology in Cur Deus Homo (c. 1098 CE). Anselm interpreted Christ's atonement as fulfilling Israel's sacrificial system, making the Church the community where this redemption is applied. He viewed the Old Testament Law as preparatory, with the Church as the perfected Israel: "The promises to Israel find their end in Christ, through whom the Church becomes the true people of God." Anselm's rational approach

Who is Israel?: A Historic Reflection of Church History

influenced later scholastics, reinforcing typology where Israel's history prefigures the Church's reality.

Bernard of Clairvaux (1090–1153 CE), a Cistercian abbot and mystic, deepened this theology through his allegorical exegesis. In his Sermons on the Song of Songs (c. 1135–1153 CE), Bernard interprets the bride as the Church, the spiritual Israel betrothed to Christ: "The Church is the true daughter of Zion, inheriting the covenant through the Bridegroom who redeems her." His writings emphasize the Church's role as a "kingdom of priests" (Exodus 19:6), fulfilled in monastic and ecclesial life. Bernard's involvement in the Second Crusade (1147 CE) reflected a complex view of Judaism, but theologically, he upheld the Church as the fulfillment of Israel's calling to holiness.

Thomas Aquinas (1225–1274 CE) represents the pinnacle of medieval scholasticism, synthesizing Aristotelian philosophy with Christian doctrine in his Summa Theologica (1265–1274 CE). Aquinas affirms the Church as the True Israel, arguing that the Old Testament promises are fulfilled spiritually in the New Covenant. In Summa Theologica (I-II, q. 103, a. 3), he states, "The Old Law was given to the Jews as a pedagogy leading to Christ; now, in the Church, the grace of Christ perfects what the Law foreshadowed." Aquinas distinguishes between the ceremonial, judicial, and moral aspects of the Law, seeing the ceremonial (e.g., sacrifices) as types fulfilled in Christ's Eucharist and the Church's sacraments. Scholars debate whether Aquinas was strictly supersessionist, but his theology emphasizes fulfillment: the Church does not replace Israel but perfects it through grace, as grace "does not destroy nature but perfects it" (Summa Theologica I, q. 1, a. 8). He interprets Romans 11:17-24 as Gentiles grafted into Israel's olive tree, making the Church the expanded covenant community.

Typology and Allegory in Medieval Exegesis

Typology and allegory were central to medieval interpretations of Scripture, allowing theologians to see the Church as the fulfillment of Old Testament promises. The fourfold sense of Scripture—literal, allegorical, moral, and anagogical—facilitated this. For instance, the Exodus was literally historical but allegorically represented Christ's redemption of the Church from sin, morally called believers to obedience, and anagogically pointed to heavenly rest. Hugh of St. Victor (1096–1141 CE), in his Didascalicon (c. 1120 CE), systematized this approach: "The Old Testament is a figure of the New; Israel's journey prefigures the Church's pilgrimage to Christ."

Medieval liturgy and art reinforced this theology. Cathedrals depicted Old Testament scenes alongside New Testament fulfillments, such as Moses striking the rock (Exodus 17:6) paralleled with Christ as the living water (John 4:14). The Glossa Ordinaria (c. 1100 CE), a standard biblical commentary, applied passages like Psalm 80 (Israel as the vine) to the Church as the true vine in Christ (John 15:1). This interpretive tradition underscored the Church's identity as the spiritual Israel, transcending the physical nation.

From Medieval to Reformation: Continuity and Renewal

The medieval period solidified the Church's identity as the True Israel, with theologians like Thomas Aquinas and Bernard of Clairvaux weaving Old Testament promises into a robust ecclesiology through typology and allegory. Their work, rooted in Augustine's vision of the Church as the City of God, affirmed that God's covenant people transcended ethnic or national boundaries, finding fulfillment in Christ's universal body. Yet, by the late medieval era, challenges to this consensus emerged. The Church's growing institutional power, coupled with theological accretions and moral failures, sparked calls for reform, setting the stage for a seismic shift in Christian thought.

The Protestant Reformation, ignited in the 16th century, did not abandon the Church-as-Israel theology but renewed it through a return to Scripture and covenantal clarity. Figures like John Wycliffe and Jan Hus, precursors to the Reformers, began questioning papal authority and emphasizing biblical authority, laying groundwork for a theology that reaffirmed the Church as the spiritual heir of Israel. As the Reformation unfolded, Martin Luther and John Calvin built on this legacy, refining medieval insights with *sola scriptura* and a sharpened focus on faith, ensuring the Church's identity as the True Israel endured in a new era.

The Reformation and Continuity

The Protestant Reformation (16th century) reaffirmed the Church's identity as the True Israel, with reformers building on the patristic and medieval tradition while emphasizing sola scriptura and covenant continuity. Rejecting Roman Catholic accretions, figures like Martin Luther and John Calvin returned to New Testament teachings, viewing the Church as the expanded Israel united by faith in Christ. This era's covenant theology rejected any notion of "replacement," instead seeing the Church as the fulfillment and continuation of God's promises to Abraham (Genesis 12:3), with Gentiles grafted into Israel's root (Romans 11:17-24). The Reformers' focus on predestination, grace, and Scripture reinforced this, countering dispensational distinctions between Israel and the Church.

Martin Luther's Contribution

Martin Luther (1483–1546 CE) was instrumental in articulating the Church as the True Israel through faith. In his Commentary on Galatians (1535 CE), Luther expounds Galatians 3:28-29: "There is neither Jew nor Greek... for if you belong to Christ, then you are Abraham's seed, and heirs according to the promise." He argues that true Israel is defined by faith, not ethnicity: "The true children of Abraham are those who believe the promise, fulfilled in Christ; the Church is thus the Israel of God" (Galatians 6:16). Luther's early work, That Jesus Christ Was Born a Jew (1523 CE), expressed sympathy for Jews, urging their conversion as part of God's plan for Israel's remnant. However, his later writings, like On the Jews and Their Lies (1543 CE), reflected anti-Judaism, complicating his legacy. Theologically, Luther upheld continuity: the Church inherits Israel's promises through Christ, the true seed.

John Calvin's Covenant Theology

John Calvin (1509–1564 CE) provided a systematic framework in his Institutes of the Christian Religion (1536–1559 CE), emphasizing the unity of the covenant. He writes, "The covenant made with all the patriarchs is so much like ours in substance and reality that the two are actually one and the same. Yet they differ in the mode of dispensation" (Institutes 2.10.2). For Calvin, the Old Testament Israel was the Church in infancy, matured in the New Testament: "The Church has always been the Israel of God, now revealed fully in Christ." In his Commentary on Romans (1540 CE), Calvin interprets Romans 9–11 as affirming a faithful remnant—Jew and Gentile—in the Church, with "all Israel" (Romans 11:26) as the elect people of God. Calvin's theology influenced Reformed confessions, like the Heidelberg Catechism (1563 CE), which applies Old Testament promises to the Church.

Virgil A. Walker

Thomas Cranmer: The Church in Liturgical Continuity

Thomas Cranmer (1489–1556), the primary author of the *Book of Common Prayer* (1549, 1552), embedded the theology of the Church as the True Israel within Anglican worship, reflecting the Reformation's commitment to sola scriptura and the continuity of God's covenant. In his *Homily of Salvation* (1547), part of the *Book of Homilies* appointed for use in the Church of England, Cranmer articulates justification by faith as the defining mark of God's people: "By faith alone, without works, we are justified... and thus the Church becomes the true seed of Abraham, inheriting the promises through Christ" (*Certain Sermons or Homilies*, 1547). This echoes Galatians 3:28–29, cited in Chapter 2, where believers, Jew and Gentile, are "Abraham's offspring, heirs according to the promise." Cranmer's theology aligns with the Lutheran insistence that faith, not ethnicity or works, defines membership in the True Israel, reinforcing this book's rejection of dispensationalism's separation of Israel and the Church.

Cranmer's liturgical work further solidifies this identity. The *Book of Common Prayer* weaves Old Testament imagery into its prayers and Eucharistic rites, portraying the Church as the fulfillment of Israel's covenant. For example, the Collect for the Second Sunday of Advent invokes Romans 15:4–13, praying that Scripture might lead the Church to "embrace and ever hold fast the blessed hope of everlasting life," a hope rooted in the promises to Abraham now fulfilled in Christ's universal body. The Eucharistic prayers draw on Passover imagery (Exodus 12), presenting Christ as the true Paschal Lamb (1 Corinthians 5:7), with the Church as the covenant community celebrating redemption. By applying titles like "royal priesthood" and "holy nation" (Exodus 19:6; 1 Peter 2:9) to the worshipping community, Cranmer's liturgy embodies the Church's role as the True Israel, uniting believers through Word and Sacrament in a manner resonant with Lutheran ecclesiology (Augsburg Confession, Article VII). This liturgical theology enriches the historical consensus traced in Chapter 4, showing how Anglican worship has long affirmed the Church's covenantal identity.

Other Reformers and Confessions

Ulrich Zwingli (1484–1531 CE) and Heinrich Bullinger (1504–1575 CE) developed covenant theology in Zurich, viewing the Church as the covenant community from Abraham onward. Bullinger's Second Helvetic Confession (1566 CE) states, "The Church is the congregation of the faithful... from Adam to the end of the world." In Scotland, John Knox (1514–1572 CE) echoed this, seeing the Kirk as the True Israel. The Westminster Confession of Faith (1646 CE), though post-Reformation, encapsulates this: "The visible Church... is the kingdom of the Lord Jesus Christ, the house and family of God" (25.2), inheriting Israel's role.

The Reformers navigated Jewish relations amid expulsions (e.g., from Spain in 1492 CE), but their theology focused on fulfillment: the Church expands Israel, fulfilling prophecies like Isaiah 49:6.

Challenges to the View

While the identification of the Church as the True Israel was dominant, it faced occasional challenges. Jewish-Christian dialogues, particularly in the medieval period, prompted theologians to grapple with the role of the Jewish people in God's plan. Figures like Aquinas and later reformers maintained that the Jews remained significant in salvation history, but they consistently affirmed the Church as the covenant community. Other challenges came from heretical movements, such as the Cathars, who rejected the Old Testament, forcing the Church to defend the continuity of God's covenant with Israel and its fulfillment in the Church.

Despite these challenges, the view of the Church as the True Israel remained the theological consensus. Even in the Eastern Orthodox tradition, theologians like John of Damascus (c. 675–749) echoed Western views, using Old Testament imagery to describe the Church as the new Israel, united in Christ's body.

Persistence Until the 19th Century

The theology of the Church as the True Israel persisted through the post-Reformation period and into the early modern era. Puritan theologians in the 17th and 18th centuries, such as John Owen, applied covenant theology to affirm the Church's identity as Israel, seeing their communities as heirs of the promises. This view dominated Christian thought until the 19th century, when new theological currents, particularly dispensationalism, began to challenge it.

Theological Implications

The historic identification of the Church as the True Israel underscores the unity of God's covenant across history. By interpreting Old Testament promises through typology and allegory, theologians affirmed that the Church fulfills Israel's spiritual calling as a "kingdom of priests" (Exodus 19:6). This theology challenges any notion that Israel's identity is tied to a secular state, emphasizing instead a spiritual community defined by faith in Christ.

Conclusion

For over a millennium, the Church consistently affirmed its identity as the True Israel, from Augustine's comprehensive theology to the Reformers' biblical exegesis, including Luther's emphasis on faith as the defining mark of God's people. Typology and allegory provided a framework for understanding the Church as the fulfillment of God's promises, despite occasional challenges. This consensus held firm until the 19th century, when dispensationalism introduced a radical shift. In the next chapter, we will explore how John Darby's theology disrupted this historic view, reshaping modern evangelical thought and its understanding of Israel.

Sources:

- Beale, G.K. A New Testament Biblical Theology: The Unfolding of the Old Testament in the New. Grand Rapids: Baker Academic, 2011.

- Augustine. City of God. Translated by Henry Bettenson. London: Penguin Classics, 2003.

- Tapie, Matthew A. Aquinas on Israel and the Church: The Question of Supersessionism in the Theology of Thomas Aquinas. Eugene: Pickwick Publications, 2014.

- Aquinas, Thomas. Summa Theologica. Translated by Fathers of the English Dominican Province. New York: Benziger Bros., 1947.

- Bernard of Clairvaux. Sermons on the Song of Songs. Translated by Kilian Walsh. Kalamazoo: Cistercian Publications, 1971.

- Anselm of Canterbury. Cur Deus Homo. Translated by Sidney Norton Deane. Chicago: Open Court Publishing, 1903.

- Luther, Martin. Commentary on Galatians. Translated by Theodore Graebner. Grand Rapids: Zondervan, 1949.

- Luther, Martin. That Jesus Christ Was Born a Jew. Translated by Martin H. Bertram. In Luther's Works, vol. 45. Philadelphia: Fortress Press, 1962.

- Calvin, John. Institutes of the Christian Religion. Translated by Henry Beveridge. Grand Rapids: Eerdmans, 1989.

- Calvin, John. Commentary on Romans. Translated by John Owen. Grand Rapids: Baker Books, 2009.

- Cranmer, Thomas. Certain Sermons or Homilies Appointed to Be Read in Churches. London: Richard Jugge and John Cawood, 1547.

- Cranmer, Thomas. The Book of Common Prayer. London: Edward Whitchurch, 1552.

- Bullinger, Heinrich. The Second Helvetic Confession. In The Creeds of Christendom, vol. 3, edited by Philip Schaff. Grand Rapids: Baker Books, 1996.

- Soulen, R. Kendall. The God of Israel and Christian Theology. Minneapolis: Fortress Press, 1996.

- Wright, N.T. Paul and the Faithfulness of God. Minneapolis: Fortress Press, 2013.

- Vlach, Michael J. Has the Church Replaced Israel? A Theological Evaluation. Nashville: B&H Academic, 2010.

Virgil A. Walker

Chapter 5: John Darby and the Rise of Dispensationalism

For over a millennium, the Christian Church consistently identified itself as the True Israel, inheriting the covenant promises of the Old Testament through faith in Christ, as traced in Chapters 1 through 4. This theological consensus, rooted in Scripture and affirmed by the early church fathers, medieval theologians, and Reformers, held that the Church, as the universal body of believers, fulfilled God's plan for His covenant people. It emphasized the continuity of God's redemptive work, where the promises to Abraham—blessing all nations (Genesis 12:3)—found their fulfillment in the inclusive community of faith, Jew and Gentile alike, united in Christ (Galatians 3:28-29). However, in the 19th century, a radical theological shift emerged through the work of John Nelson Darby, whose dispensationalist framework separated Israel and the Church as distinct entities in God's plan. This innovation not only challenged the historic unity of covenant theology but also introduced a fragmented view of salvation history, treating the Church as a mere interlude in God's dealings with national Israel.

This chapter examines Darby's innovations, the historical context that shaped them, their dissemination through influential channels like the Scofield Reference Bible, and their profound impact on modern evangelical Christianity, particularly in the United States. It also explores the political and cultural ramifications of dispensationalism, including the rise of Christian Zionism, and critiques this theology from traditional perspectives, arguing that it deviates from the biblical and historical understanding of the Church as the True Israel. By dissecting dispensationalism's origins, doctrines, and consequences, we will highlight how this minority view—despite its popularity—represents a departure from the apostolic and patristic consensus, often driven by cultural anxieties rather than exegetical fidelity. Ultimately, this analysis underscores the need to reclaim the Church's historic identity, rejecting dispensationalism's dualistic framework in favor of the unified covenantal narrative presented in Scripture.

The Historical Context of Dispensationalism

The 19th century was a period of significant theological, social, and political change, providing fertile ground for new ideas like dispensationalism. The Industrial Revolution disrupted traditional societies, fostering urbanization, economic inequality, and a sense of eschatological urgency among believers who saw these upheavals as signs of the end times. Scientific advancements, such as Charles Darwin's theory of evolution (published in 1859), and the Enlightenment's emphasis on rationalism and empiricism challenged traditional Christian doctrines, prompting varied responses within the Church. Liberal theology,

Virgil A. Walker

exemplified by figures like Friedrich Schleiermacher and Albrecht Ritschl, sought to accommodate faith to modern science and culture, often at the expense of supernatural elements like miracles and prophecy. In reaction, conservative evangelicals emphasized biblical inerrancy and literal interpretation, creating an environment ripe for innovative eschatological systems.

In Britain, the Established Church (Church of England) faced criticism from dissenting groups, including the Plymouth Brethren, a movement with which John Nelson Darby (1800–1882) was closely associated. The Brethren, emerging in the 1820s in Dublin and Plymouth, emphasized a return to biblical literalism, simple church gatherings without formal clergy, and a rejection of institutional religion. This reflected a broader evangelical revival, influenced by the Second Great Awakening in America and the prophetic conferences in Britain, which sought to counter liberal theology and secularism. The apocalyptic fervor of the time—fueled by events like the French Revolution (1789–1799), the Napoleonic Wars (1803–1815), and the Irish Potato Famine (1845–1852)—intensified interest in end-times prophecy. Millenarian movements, such as the Adventists, speculated on Christ's imminent return, drawing from Daniel and Revelation.

Darby, an Anglican clergyman turned Brethren leader, developed his theological system in this context of religious ferment. Born in London to an Anglo-Irish family, Darby studied at Trinity College, Dublin, and was ordained in 1825. His early ministry in rural Ireland exposed him to Catholic-Protestant tensions and social upheaval, including the push for Catholic emancipation (achieved in 1829), which he viewed as a betrayal of Protestant principles. Disillusioned with the state church's entanglement with politics, Darby resigned in 1827 and joined the Brethren, where he honed his ideas during annual Bible conferences. His experiences may have shaped his emphasis on a distinct plan for Israel, reflecting a desire to anchor God's promises in a literal, historical fulfillment amid perceived cultural decline. As historian Timothy P. Weber notes, "Dispensationalism arose as a response to the perceived failures of postmillennial optimism, offering a pessimistic view of history that aligned with the era's crises." This context not only birthed dispensationalism but also ensured its appeal to those seeking certainty in uncertain times.

John Darby and the Dispensational Framework

John Nelson Darby's dispensationalism introduced a novel approach to biblical interpretation, dividing history into distinct "dispensations" or periods in which God deals with humanity in different ways. Typically numbering seven (e.g., Innocence, Conscience, Human Government, Promise, Law, Grace, and Kingdom), these dispensations framed God's interactions as progressive tests of obedience, each ending in failure except the final millennial kingdom. Central to Darby's theology was the separation of Israel and the Church as two distinct peoples with separate divine purposes. Unlike the historic view, which saw the Church as the fulfillment of Israel's covenant promises (as articulated by Paul in Romans 11 and Galatians 3), Darby argued that Israel (understood as the ethnic Jewish people and nation) remained God's chosen people with unfulfilled promises, particularly regarding the land, temple, and a future millennial kingdom. The Church, in his view, was a "parenthesis" or "heavenly mystery" in God's plan—a temporary entity revealed only in the New Testament (Ephesians 3:1-6)—to be removed via the rapture before God resumes His work with national Israel during the tribulation and millennium.

Darby's key theological innovations included:

- Premillennialism: The belief that Christ will return before a literal 1,000-year reign on earth, during which Israel will be restored as a nation and rule from Jerusalem (Revelation 20:1–6). Unlike historic premillennialism (held by some early fathers like Irenaeus), which integrated the Church as central to the kingdom, Darby's version emphasized Israel's national restoration, with converted Jews evangelizing the world during the millennium. He drew from Daniel 9:24-27, interpreting the "seventy weeks" as prophetic years, with the final week (the tribulation) postponed until after the Church age.

Who is Israel?: A Historic Reflection of Church History

- The Rapture: Darby popularized the idea of a secret, pretribulational rapture, where believers are "caught up" to heaven before the tribulation (1 Thessalonians 4:17). This doctrine, absent from historic theology, separated the Church's destiny (a heavenly inheritance) from Israel's earthly promises. In his writings, such as The Hopes of the Church of God (1840), Darby argued, "The Church is not of the world... it will be taken out of it before the judgments come."

- Literalist Hermeneutics: Darby advocated a strictly literal interpretation of Old Testament prophecies, rejecting the typological and allegorical methods of the early church (e.g., Origen) and Reformers (e.g., Calvin). For example, he interpreted promises of land to Abraham (Genesis 12:7; 15:18) as applying eternally to a future Jewish state, not spiritually to the Church. This "literal where possible" approach dismissed New Testament reapplications of Old Testament texts (e.g., Amos 9:11-12 in Acts 15:16-18) as secondary, preserving a dual track for Israel and the Church.

These ideas were disseminated through Darby's extensive writings (over 30 volumes), sermons, and travels. His seven visits to North America between 1862 and 1877 influenced evangelical leaders at Bible conferences, such as those in Niagara-on-the-Lake, where dispensationalism gained foothold among fundamentalists. Darby's emphasis on ecclesiology—simple gatherings without clergy—complemented his eschatology, portraying the Church as a "ruin" awaiting rapture, which resonated with disillusioned believers.

The Dangers of Non-Denominationalism

Dispensationalism's rise coincided with the growth of non-denominationalism, particularly within the Plymouth Brethren and later evangelical movements, which further distanced believers from the historic and catholic roots of the Church. Non-denominationalism, often aligned with dispensationalist thought, rejects formal ecclesiastical structures, creeds, and traditions, claiming to return to a "pure" New Testament model of Christianity. However, this rejection severs the Church from its historical continuity, undermining the catholicity—the universal, unified witness—of the faith across time and cultures. The early church fathers, such as Ignatius of Antioch (d. 108) and Irenaeus (d. 202), emphasized the importance of apostolic succession and tradition to safeguard sound doctrine against heresy. By contrast, non-denominationalism's dismissal of tradition often results in a rootless Christianity, disconnected from the historical struggles, councils, and martyrs who defended the faith against heresies like Gnosticism and Arianism.

This disconnection from the Church's history fosters a theological amnesia, where the sacrifices and wisdom of past generations are forgotten. Non-denominational churches, in their pursuit of simplicity and independence, often neglect the rich legacy of creeds (e.g., Nicene, Apostles'), confessions, and liturgical practices that have anchored Christian identity for centuries. As Jaroslav Pelikan notes in *The Vindication of Tradition* (1984), "Tradition is the living faith of the dead; traditionalism is the dead faith of the living." By discarding tradition, non-denominationalism risks reducing Christianity to individual interpretation and contemporary relevance, ignoring the communal and historical dimensions of the faith. This approach fails to honor the memory of our brethren—those who faced persecution, clarified doctrine through councils (e.g., Nicaea in 325, Chalcedon in 451), and preserved the gospel through centuries of trial.

Moreover, non-denominationalism's lack of reliance on the broader Church community weakens its ability to maintain doctrinal coherence. Without accountability to historic confessions or ecclesiastical oversight, these communities are susceptible to theological fads, such as dispensationalism's speculative eschatology, which thrive in environments unmoored from tradition. The emphasis on individual Bible study and literalist hermeneutics, while well-intentioned, often overlooks the interpretive wisdom of the Church fathers and Reformers, leading to novel doctrines like the rapture that lack historical precedent. This isolation from the Church's catholicity—its unity across time, place, and culture—diminishes the sense of belonging to a universal body, replacing it with fragmented, local expressions of faith that prioritize personal experience over collective heritage.

Virgil A. Walker

The Scofield Reference Bible and Widespread Influence

Dispensationalism gained widespread traction through the Scofield Reference Bible (1909, revised 1917), edited by Cyrus Ingerson Scofield (1843–1921), a lawyer-turned-pastor and disciple of Darby's teachings via American evangelists like Dwight L. Moody. This study Bible, published by Oxford University Press, featured the King James Version text alongside extensive notes, charts, and cross-references that embedded dispensationalism into Scripture. Scofield's annotations explicitly separated Israel and the Church, presenting Old Testament prophecies as applying to a future Jewish nation rather than the Church. For instance, his note on Genesis 12:1-3 states, "The Abrahamic Covenant... is unconditional and depends upon God's faithfulness, not Israel's," implying unfulfilled promises for ethnic Israel. Similarly, notes on Romans 11 and Revelation 7 emphasize a distinct role for 144,000 Jewish evangelists in the end times, reinforcing Darby's dualism.

The Scofield Reference Bible was immensely popular, selling millions of copies and becoming a staple in evangelical homes, churches, and seminaries. Its accessibility—clear notes for lay readers—and authoritative tone made dispensationalism mainstream within evangelicalism, particularly among fundamentalists reacting against modernist theology (e.g., the 1910–1915 Fundamentals series). Institutions like Moody Bible

Who is Israel?: A Historic Reflection of Church History

Institute (founded 1886) and Dallas Theological Seminary (founded 1924 by Lewis Sperry Chafer, a Scofield protégé) further institutionalized dispensationalism, training generations of pastors in its principles. Chafer's Systematic Theology (1947–1948) codified it, influencing figures like John Walvoord and Charles Ryrie, whose works (e.g., Ryrie's Dispensationalism Today, 1965) defended it against critics.

The Rise of Christian Zionism

Dispensationalism's emphasis on a restored Jewish nation fueled the rise of Christian Zionism, the belief that the modern state of Israel is a fulfillment of biblical prophecy and must be supported to hasten Christ's return. While Jewish Zionism, led by Theodor Herzl (1860–1904) and formalized at the 1897 Basel Congress, was a secular nationalist movement responding to anti-Semitism, dispensationalists provided a theological overlay. Darby's literalism aligned with early Zionist efforts, such as the Balfour Declaration (1917), which promised a Jewish homeland in Palestine. William E. Blackstone's Jesus is Coming (1878) and the 1891 Blackstone Memorial petitioned U.S. President Benjamin Harrison to support Jewish return to Palestine, echoing dispensationalist hopes.

The establishment of Israel in 1948 and the Six-Day War in 1967, where Israel captured Jerusalem, were hailed as prophetic fulfillments by dispensationalists. Hal Lindsey's The Late Great Planet Earth (1970), selling over 35 million copies, interpreted these events through Ezekiel 36–37 (the valley of dry bones) and Zechariah 14, portraying Israel as central to end-times prophecy. Christian Zionism has had significant political implications, particularly in the United States. Evangelical leaders like Jerry Falwell (founder of the Moral Majority in 1979) and Pat Robertson (700 Club) advocated strong support for Israel, influencing policies under presidents like Ronald Reagan and Donald Trump. Organizations such as Christians United for Israel (CUFI), founded in 2006 by John Hagee, mobilize millions of evangelicals, lobbying for U.S. aid to Israel (over $3 billion annually) and opposing Palestinian statehood. This alignment has often blurred theology and geopolitics, with dispensationalism providing a biblical rationale for activism, sometimes at the expense of peacemaking or Palestinian Christian perspectives.

Effects on Modern Evangelical Christianity

Dispensationalism's impact on modern evangelicalism is profound, particularly in the United States, where it shapes eschatology, preaching, and culture. By separating Israel and the Church, it shifted focus toward prophecy charts, end-times speculation, and a pessimistic view of history, portraying the Church age as declining toward apostasy. Popular media like Lindsey's book and the Left Behind series (1995–2007, over 65 million copies sold) embedded the rapture and Israel's restoration in evangelical imagination, influencing worship (e.g., songs about the rapture) and missions (prioritizing evangelism before the tribulation).

Theologically, dispensationalism has created a dualistic framework, emphasizing a future role for national Israel over the Church's present identity as the covenant community. This has led to a diminished emphasis on social justice, environmental stewardship, and kingdom-building, as believers await escape via rapture. Politically, it has aligned evangelicals with conservative causes, including unwavering support for Israel, contributing to the Religious Right's rise in the 1980s. In media, outlets like Trinity Broadcasting Network promote dispensationalist teachers, while seminaries like Dallas Theological continue its legacy. Globally, dispensationalism has spread through missions, influencing churches in Latin America and Africa, though it remains a minority view in historic denominations like Anglicanism, Lutheran, and Presbyterianism. Estimating the percentage of Christians worldwide who are dispensationalist is challenging due to limited global data and varying definitions of dispensationalism. However, A rough estimate suggests that no more than 10%-15% of Christians worldwide adhere to dispensationalist beliefs, with the majority of these in the U.S. While influential in American evangelicalism, is less common globally due to its historical roots in 19th-century America and limited adoption in other regions like Europe, Africa, or Asia, where other theological frameworks dominate.

Virgil A. Walker

Critiques from Traditional Perspectives

Dispensationalism has faced significant criticism from traditional and covenantal theologians for its departure from historic Christian theology. Critics argue that its separation of Israel and the Church undermines the unity of God's covenant, as articulated by Paul: "There is neither Jew nor Greek... for you are all one in Christ Jesus" (Galatians 3:28). Theologians like N.T. Wright (in Paul and the Faithfulness of God, 2013) and George Eldon Ladd (in The Presence of the Future, 1974) contend that dispensationalism's literalist hermeneutics misinterprets Old Testament prophecies, ignoring their New Testament fulfillment in Christ and the Church. For example, Wright argues that passages like Romans 11 envision "all Israel" as the full elect people—Jew and Gentile—saved through faith, not a national restoration apart from the Church.

Covenantal theologians, such as those in the Reformed tradition (e.g., O. Palmer Robertson in The Christ of the Covenants, 1980), critique dispensationalism for fragmenting salvation history into disconnected dispensations, contrary to the unified covenant theology of Augustine and Calvin. They challenge the rapture doctrine as a 19th-century innovation, noting that 1 Thessalonians 4:17 describes a public descent of Christ, not a secret removal, and parallels the parousia in Matthew 24:30-31. Furthermore, critics highlight the political implications of Christian Zionism, arguing that it risks conflating biblical promises with modern geopolitics, potentially sidelining the Church's universal mission and ignoring the suffering of Palestinian Christians. As R. Kendall Soulen warns in The God of Israel and Christian Theology (1996), dispensationalism's dualism can inadvertently foster supersessionism in reverse, elevating ethnic Israel over the Church.

Theological Implications

Dispensationalism's separation of Israel and the Church represents a radical departure from the historic view that the Church is the True Israel. By prioritizing a national restoration of Israel, it diminishes the Church's identity as the covenant community, creating a theological dualism that contrasts with the New Testament's emphasis on unity in Christ (Ephesians 2:11-22). Its influence on evangelicalism has reshaped preaching (focusing on prophecy over discipleship), eschatology (promoting escapism), and political engagement (aligning with Zionism), often overshadowing the historic consensus traced in previous chapters. This shift not only obscures the Church's role as the fulfillment of Abraham's seed but also risks politicizing faith, equating God's kingdom with earthly nations rather than the spiritual body of believers.

Conclusion

John Nelson Darby's dispensationalism, amplified by the Scofield Reference Bible and Christian Zionism, introduced a seismic shift in Christian theology, challenging the historic identification of the Church as the True Israel. Emerging from 19th-century crises, its doctrines of separate dispensations, pretribulational rapture, and literalist hermeneutics fragmented God's unified covenant plan, prioritizing a future for national Israel over the Church's present calling. While influential, particularly among American evangelicals through popular media and political activism, this minority view diverges from the biblical and historical consensus, often driven by cultural pessimism rather than exegetical depth. In the concluding chapter, we will summarize the evidence for the Church as the True Israel and urge Christians to reject dispensationalism's distortions, reclaiming their historic identity as God's covenant people united in faith.

Sources:

- Bass, Clarence B. Backgrounds to Dispensationalism: Its Historical Genesis and Ecclesiastical Implications. Grand Rapids: Eerdmans, 1960.

- Weber, Timothy P. On the Road to Armageddon: How Evangelicals Became Israel's Best Friend. Grand Rapids: Baker Academic, 2004.

- Sizer, Stephen. Christian Zionism: Road-map to Armageddon? Downers Grove: InterVarsity Press, 2004.

- Ryrie, Charles C. Dispensationalism Today. Chicago: Moody Press, 1965.

- Darby, John Nelson. The Collected Writings of J.N. Darby. Edited by William Kelly. Stow Hill: Bible and Tract Depot, 1867–1883.

- Scofield, Cyrus I. The Scofield Reference Bible. New York: Oxford University Press, 1909.

- Lindsey, Hal. The Late Great Planet Earth. Grand Rapids: Zondervan, 1970.

- Wright, N.T. Paul and the Faithfulness of God. Minneapolis: Fortress Press, 2013.

- Ladd, George Eldon. The Presence of the Future: The Eschatology of Biblical Realism. Grand Rapids: Eerdmans, 1974.

- Robertson, O. Palmer. The Christ of the Covenants. Phillipsburg: Presbyterian and Reformed Publishing, 1980.

- Soulen, R. Kendall. The God of Israel and Christian Theology. Minneapolis: Fortress Press, 1996.

- Chafer, Lewis Sperry. Systematic Theology. Dallas: Dallas Seminary Press, 1947–1948.

- Vlach, Michael J. *Has the Church Replaced Israel? A Theological Evaluation.* Nashville: B&H Academic, 2010.

Conclusion: Reclaiming the True Israel

The question "Who is Israel?" is not merely a theological curiosity but a matter of profound significance for the Christian faith, shaping how believers understand their identity as God's covenant people. Throughout this book, we have traced the biblical and historical evidence demonstrating that the True Israel is the Church—the universal community of faith in Jesus Christ, not a secular state or ethnic nation. From the multifaceted identity of Israel in the Old Testament to the transformative redefinition through Christ's coming, the early church's consensus, and the historic theology of the medieval and Reformation periods, the Church has consistently been recognized as the heir of God's covenant promises. Yet, in the 19th century, John Nelson Darby's dispensationalism introduced a radical departure, separating Israel and the Church and reshaping evangelical thought. This conclusion summarizes these findings, argues that dispensationalism is a theological heresy or heterodox at best, that robs Christians of their true identity, and urges believers to return to the historic roots of embracing the Church as the True Israel.

Summarizing the Biblical and Historical Evidence

Virgil A. Walker

Our journey began in the Old Testament (Chapter 1), where Israel emerged as both a nation and a covenant community defined by faith. The promises to Abraham (Genesis 12:1–3) and the calling at Sinai (Exodus 19:5–6) established Israel as a "kingdom of priests," with hints of inclusivity for faithful Gentiles (Isaiah 56:6–8). This dual identity—national yet spiritual—set the stage for a broader understanding of God's people. In Chapter 2, we saw how Jesus' life, death, and resurrection fulfilled these promises, redefining Israel as a universal community of faith. Through passages like Galatians 3:28–29 and Ephesians 2:11–22, the New Testament presents the Church as the "new Israel," where faith in Christ, not ethnicity, defines membership.

The early church fathers, as explored in Chapter 3, solidified this understanding. Figures like Justin Martyr, Irenaeus, Origen, and Augustine affirmed the Church as the True Israel, using typology and allegory to interpret Old Testament promises as fulfilled in Christ's body. The destruction of the Temple in 70 CE further reinforced this shift, marking the transition from a national to a spiritual covenant community. Chapter 4 traced this theology through the medieval period and Reformation, with theologians like Aquinas, Luther, and Calvin emphasizing the unity of God's covenant. Luther's assertion that the true Israel is defined "not by physical descent from Abraham, but by faith in the promise, which is fulfilled in Christ" (Commentary on Galatians, 1535) encapsulates this historic consensus, which persisted until the 19th century.

Chapter 5 examined the disruption caused by John Nelson Darby's dispensationalism, which separated Israel and the Church as distinct entities in God's plan. Through the Scofield Reference Bible and the rise of Christian Zionism, dispensationalism became a mainstream influence in evangelicalism, aligning support for the modern state of Israel with biblical prophecy. However, this minority view diverges sharply from the historic theology that unites God's covenant across history in the Church.

The identification of the Church as the True Israel is not only a matter of historical and biblical fidelity but also a lens through which Christians understand their eschatological hope and missional calling. By embracing their identity as the covenant people, believers are anchored in the certainty of Christ's return, not as a speculative event tied to geopolitical developments, but as the consummation of God's kingdom, where the Church—Jew and Gentile united—reigns with Christ (Revelation 5:9-10). This eschatological vision empowers the Church to live out its calling as a "light to the nations" (Isaiah 42:6), embodying justice, mercy, and reconciliation in a fractured world. The True Israel is not a passive entity awaiting escape but an active community, proclaiming the gospel and advancing God's kingdom through love and service, fulfilling the Abrahamic promise to bless all nations (Genesis 12:3).

The Heterodoxy of Dispensationalism— Leaning Toward Heresy

Dispensationalism is not merely a theological alternative but a serious heterodox innovation, leaning toward heresy in its effects. Though not damnable (Galatians 1:8–9), it gravely undermines Christian identity by splitting God's people into two tracks—ethnic Israel and the Church—contradicting the New Testament's unity: "there is neither Jew nor Greek... for you are all one in Christ Jesus" (Galatians 3:28).

This dualism robs believers of their birthright as Abraham's heirs (Romans 11:17–24), relegating the Church to a mere parenthesis while exalting a future national entity over the spiritual reality fulfilled in Christ—the Lamb who takes away the sin of the world (John 1:29) and the true temple in whom we now dwell (John 2:19–21; 1 Corinthians 3:16).

Moreover, dispensationalism's literalist hermeneutics misinterpret Old Testament prophecies, ignoring their spiritual fulfillment in the Church, as affirmed by centuries of exegesis from Augustine to Calvin. Its doctrines, such as the rapture and a future millennial kingdom centered on ethnic Israel, lack biblical grounding and represent 19th-century innovations, not apostolic teaching. The political implications of dispensationalism, particularly through Christian Zionism, further complicate its errors, conflating God's covenant with modern geopolitics and sidelining the Church's universal mission to proclaim Christ to all nations (Matthew 28:19–20).

A Call to Return to Historic Roots

The evidence presented in this book compels Christians to reject dispensationalism and return to the historic roots of the Church being a unified body in bondage to Christ. The Church is the True Israel, the community of believers—Jew and Gentile—united in Christ, who fulfills the Law and the Prophets (Matthew 5:17). This theology, grounded in Scripture and affirmed across centuries, offers a unified vision of God's redemptive plan, restoring the Church's identity as the covenant people called to be a "royal priesthood" and a "holy nation" (1 Peter 2:9). By embracing this truth, Christians can reclaim their calling to reflect God's glory and extend His grace to the world.

Implications for Today

The reclamation of the Church as the True Israel is not a retreat into theological abstraction but a call to action. In a world marked by division and conflict, the Church must embody its identity as a unified, universal community, transcending national and ethnic boundaries. This identity challenges Christians to resist the politicization of faith, particularly the alignment of biblical prophecy with modern state agendas. In today's cultural landscape, the Church faces new challenges that underscore the urgency of this reclamation. The proliferation of media-driven prophecy culture, fueled by books, films, and television ministries, often perpetuates dispensationalism's speculative timelines, diverting attention from the Church's present mission. This obsession with end-times scenarios risks reducing faith to a checklist of signs rather than a vibrant relationship with Christ. Moreover, the polarization of political theology—where support for modern Israel is equated with biblical faithfulness—complicates the Church's witness, alienating those who seek a gospel unentangled with nationalism. The marginalization of covenant theology in popular Christianity, overshadowed by dispensationalist frameworks in seminaries and pulpits, further obscures the Church's unified identity. By rejecting these distortions, Christians can refocus on their calling to be a covenant community, embodying God's love across ethnic, cultural, and political divides, and engaging the world with a gospel that transcends temporal agendas.

This theological error has had seismic real-world consequences, especially in the United States. Dispensationalism's elevation of a secular Jewish state as the centerpiece of God's plan has fused evangelical piety with U.S. foreign policy. Since 1948, the U.S. has sent over $300 billion (inflation-adjusted) in aid to Israel—more than to any other nation—with $3.8 billion annually in military aid locked in through 2028 (per the 2016 MOU). This is not mere diplomacy; it is theological lobbying in action. Groups like AIPAC and Christians

Who is Israel?: A Historic Reflection of Church History

United for Israel (CUFI)—led by dispensationalist pastors like John Hagee—have built a political machine that equates criticism of Israeli policy with anti-God rebellion. In their eyes, the modern state of Israel holds an unlimited "get-out-of-jail-free" card: settlement expansion, blockade of Gaza, or military actions are waved through as "prophetic necessity," shielded from moral scrutiny by misapplied verses (e.g., Genesis 12:3 twisted into "support the government or be cursed").

This contradicts the Church's biblical mandate to advocate for God's justice in the world. The prophets thundered against oppression: *"Let justice roll down like waters, and righteousness like an ever-flowing stream"* (Amos 5:24); *"Do justice, love mercy, walk humbly with your God"* (Micah 6:8). The Church, as the True Israel, is called to speak truth to power, not grant blank-check immunity to any state—secular or otherwise. When evangelical leaders lobby Congress to fund policies that displace Palestinian Christians (whose churches trace to Pentecost) or ignore war crimes, they betray the gospel of the Lamb who takes away the sin of the world (John 1:29), not just one nation. This is not anti-Semitism; it is pro-justice, pro-gospel, and pro-Church.

Yet this distortion also robs the Church of mission. Billions funneled to a geopolitical agenda could fund global orphan care, clean water, or Bible translation—actual kingdom work. Instead, prophecy conferences sell fear, not faith. The answer is not withdrawal but reclamation: teach theology rooted in God's covenant in pulpits, host justice forums with Palestinian and Messianic voices, and redirect tithes to gospel advance. The Church must model reconciliation, not tribalism.

Reclaiming the Church as the True Israel also requires a renewed approach to Jewish-Christian relations in the modern era. Believers should engage Jewish communities with humility. By fostering dialogue grounded in mutual respect and the shared hope of redemption, Christians can affirm the Church's universal calling while honoring the Jewish people as *"beloved for the sake of their forefathers"* (Romans 11:28). This approach not only counters dispensationalism's dualism but also models the reconciling love of Christ, inviting all into the covenant community.

A Pastoral Appeal for Unity and Hope

To every believer reading these words, know that your identity as part of the True Israel is a source of profound hope and purpose. In a world divided by conflict, ideology, and uncertainty, the Church stands as God's covenant community, a beacon of unity and love. You are part of a story that began with Abraham, was fulfilled in Christ, and continues through the Spirit's work in the Church today. Let this truth anchor you in times of doubt, inspire you in moments of weariness, and compel you to live out your calling as a member of God's "royal priesthood" (1 Peter 2:9). The promise of God's kingdom is not deferred to a distant future or tied to a single nation;

it is alive in you, the Church, as you worship, serve, and proclaim the gospel to all nations.

Final Exhortation

The Church stands at a crossroads. Dispensationalism, though influential, is a theological aberration that obscures the biblical and historical truth of the Church as the True Israel. Christians must reject this heresy, not out of malice, but out of fidelity to the gospel. This call demands practical action from believers and congregations alike. First, churches must prioritize the study of Scripture through the lens of historical context and purpose, teaching congregants to see the unity of God's plan from Genesis to Revelation. Bible studies, sermons, and theological education should emphasize the Church's role as the heir of Abraham's promises, countering dispensationalist distortions with sound exegesis. Second, believers should foster ecumenical unity, building bridges across denominations to reflect the universal nature of the Church as a "holy nation" (1 Peter 2:9). This unity can be expressed through shared worship, service projects, and dialogues that affirm the Church's diverse yet singular identity in Christ. Finally, Christians must engage in missions that embody the Abrahamic call to bless all nations, supporting global outreach that prioritizes gospel proclamation and justice over geopolitical agendas. By taking these steps, the Church can live out its identity as the True Israel, a community of faith, hope, and love, reflecting the glory of God to all the earth.

Virgil A. Walker

Call to Action

Thank you for reading my book! If you enjoyed it, please consider leaving a review. Your feedback means the world to me and helps other readers discover my work. Just a few words about your experience can make a big difference! Join My Reader Community for Exclusive Updates! Go to virgilawalkerbooks.com

Virgil A. Walker

About the Author

Virgil A. Walker is a passionate scholar and follower of Christ, deeply rooted in the rich soil of Lutheran theology, particularly its emphasis on justification by faith, and drawn to the reverent beauty of Anglican liturgy. Virgil seeks to balance reason, spirituality, and a commitment to the Church's unity without compromising its essentials. Virgil believes the Church must embody God's reign (Matthew 6:33), pursuing justice, mercy, and humility while resisting schism as a wound to Christ's body.

Glossary

- **Abrahamic Covenant**: The covenant God made with Abraham in Genesis 12:1–3, promising to make him a great nation, bless him, and bless all nations through his offspring. Central to the book's argument that the Church fulfills this covenant as the True Israel.

- **Allegory**: A method of biblical interpretation, prominent in the early church and medieval period, where Old Testament narratives are seen as symbolically pointing to Christ and the Church (e.g., Israel as the vine in Psalm 80 symbolizing the Church in John 15:1).

- **Arianism**: A 4th-century theological heresy, named after Arius of Alexandria (c. 250–336 CE), which denied the full divinity of Jesus Christ, asserting that the Son was a created being, subordinate to the Father, and not co-eternal or consubstantial (homoousios) with Him. Condemned at the Council of Nicaea (325 CE), Arianism challenged the early Church's Trinitarian theology, prompting robust defenses from figures like Gregory of Nazianzus, who affirmed the Church as the True Israel united by faith in the divine Christ (Theological Orations). Arianism's influence persisted in semi-Arian forms, notably affecting theologians like Eusebius of Caesarea, but was ultimately rejected in favor of Nicene orthodoxy.

- **Birkat HaMinim**: A Jewish synagogue prayer from around 90 CE, cursing "heretics," often interpreted as targeting Christians, marking a formal separation between Judaism and early Christianity.

- **Christian Zionism**: A modern evangelical movement, rooted in dispensationalism, that supports the modern state of Israel as a fulfillment of biblical prophecy, believing it hastens Christ's return.

- **Covenant**: A binding relational agreement between God and His people, foundational to Israel's identity in the Old Testament (e.g., Abrahamic, Mosaic, Davidic covenants) and fulfilled in the New Covenant through Christ.

- **Covenant Theology**: A theological framework emphasizing the unity of God's redemptive plan across history, viewing the Church as the continuation of Israel's covenant promises, in contrast to dispensationalism.

- **Dispensationalism**: A 19th-century theological system, developed by John Nelson Darby, dividing history into distinct periods (dispensations) and separating Israel and the Church as two peoples with distinct divine plans.

- **Economic Supersessionism**: A theological view that the old covenant with Israel was preparatory and fulfilled in the new covenant through Christ and the Church, emphasizing continuity rather than replacement.

- **Eschatology**: The study of end times, including Christ's return, the resurrection, and the final judgment. Dispensationalism emphasizes a premillennial eschatology with a focus on Israel's restoration.

- **Fulfillment Theology**: The view that the Church fulfills, rather than replaces, the promises made to Israel, expanding the covenant to include all believers through faith in Christ.

- **Merneptah Stele**: An Egyptian inscription from c. 1208 BCE, providing the earliest extra-biblical reference to "Israel" as a people group in Canaan, supporting the historical emergence of Israel.

- **Mosaic Covenant**: The covenant established through Moses at Sinai (Exodus 19:5–6), defining Israel as a "kingdom of priests" and a "holy nation," contingent on obedience to God's law.

- **New Covenant**: Prophesied in Jeremiah 31:31–34 and fulfilled in Christ (Luke 22:20), characterized by God's law written on the heart, uniting Jew and Gentile in the Church.

- **Premillennialism**: The belief that Christ will return before a literal 1,000-year reign (Revelation 20:1–6). Dispensational premillennialism emphasizes Israel's national restoration during this period.

- **Postmillennialism**: A theological view that Christ will return after a long period (often symbolic) of Christian influence and societal transformation, during which the gospel progressively advances, leading to a golden age of righteousness before the second coming. Contrasts with premillennialism and amillennialism.

- **Rapture**: A dispensationalist doctrine, popularized by Darby, teaching that believers will be secretly "caught up" to heaven before a tribulation period (based on 1 Thessalonians 4:17).

- **Remnant**: A biblical concept, especially in the prophets (e.g., Isaiah 10:20–22), referring to a faithful subset of Israel preserved by God. The New Testament applies this to the Church as believers in Christ (Romans 11:5).

- **Replacement Theology**: A term often used by critics to describe the view that the Church replaces Israel, though the book argues for "fulfillment theology," emphasizing the Church's expansion of Israel's covenant.

- **Scofield Reference Bible**: A 1909 study Bible by Cyrus I. Scofield, embedding dispensationalist theology through notes and charts, significantly influencing evangelical views on Israel and the Church.

- **Sola Scriptura**: A Reformation principle meaning "Scripture alone," emphasizing the Bible as the ultimate authority, used by Reformers like Luther and Calvin to affirm the Church as the True Israel.

- **True Israel**: The central thesis of the book, identifying the Church as the universal community of believers—Jew and Gentile—united by faith in Christ, fulfilling the covenant promises to Israel.

- **Typology**: A method of biblical interpretation seeing Old Testament events, figures, or institutions (e.g., the Temple, Passover) as prefiguring Christ and the Church, widely used by early church fathers and Reformers.

Bibliography

- Anselm of Canterbury. *Cur Deus Homo*. Translated by Sidney Norton Deane. Chicago: Open Court Publishing, 1903.

- Apostolic Constitutions. In *Ante-Nicene Fathers*, vol. 7, edited by Alexander Roberts and James Donaldson. Peabody: Hendrickson Publishers, 1994.

- Augustine. *City of God*. Translated by Henry Bettenson. London: Penguin Classics, 2003.

- Basil the Great. *On the Holy Spirit*. Translated by Stephen Hildebrand. Crestwood: St. Vladimir's Seminary Press, 2011.

- Bass, Clarence B. *Backgrounds to Dispensationalism: Its Historical Genesis and Ecclesiastical Implications*. Grand Rapids: Eerdmans, 1960.

- Beale, G.K. *A New Testament Biblical Theology: The Unfolding of the Old Testament in the New*. Grand Rapids: Baker Academic, 2011.

- Ben-Tor, Amnon, ed. *The Archaeology of Ancient Israel*. New Haven: Yale University Press, 1992.

- Bernard of Clairvaux. *Sermons on the Song of Songs.* Translated by Kilian Walsh. Kalamazoo: Cistercian Publications, 1971.
- Bullinger, Heinrich. *The Second Helvetic Confession.* In *The Creeds of Christendom*, vol. 3, edited by Philip Schaff. Grand Rapids: Baker Books, 1996.
- Calvin, John. *Commentary on Romans.* Translated by John Owen. Grand Rapids: Baker Books, 2009.
- Calvin, John. *Institutes of the Christian Religion.* Translated by Henry Beveridge. Grand Rapids: Eerdmans, 1989.
- Chafer, Lewis Sperry. *Systematic Theology.* Dallas: Dallas Seminary Press, 1947–1948.
- Cranmer, Thomas. Certain Sermons or Homilies Appointed to Be Read in Churches. London: Richard Jugge and John Cawood, 1547.
- Cranmer, Thomas. *The Book of Common Prayer.* London: Edward Whitchurch, 1552.
- Darby, John Nelson. *The Collected Writings of J.N. Darby.* Edited by William Kelly. Stow Hill: Bible and Tract Depot, 1867–1883.
- Dever, William G. *Who Were the Early Israelites and Where Did They Come From?* Grand Rapids: Eerdmans, 2003.

- Dunn, James D.G. *The Theology of Paul the Apostle.* Grand Rapids: Eerdmans, 1998.

- Eusebius. *Ecclesiastical History.* Translated by Kirsopp Lake. Cambridge: Harvard University Press, 1926.

- Finkelstein, Israel, and Neil Asher Silberman. *The Bible Unearthed: Archaeology's New Vision of Ancient Israel and the Origin of Its Sacred Texts.* New York: Free Press, 2001.

- Goldingay, John. *Old Testament Theology: Israel's Gospel.* Downers Grove: InterVarsity Press, 2003.

- Hasel, Michael G. "Israel in the Merneptah Stele." *Bulletin of the American Schools of Oriental Research* 296 (1994): 45–61.

- Hays, Richard B. *Echoes of Scripture in the Letters of Paul.* New Haven: Yale University Press, 1989.

- Holmes, Michael W. *The Apostolic Fathers: Greek Texts and English Translations.* Grand Rapids: Baker Academic, 2007.

- Irenaeus. *Against Heresies.* In *Ante-Nicene Fathers*, vol. 1, edited by Alexander Roberts and James Donaldson. Peabody: Hendrickson Publishers, 1994.

- Justin Martyr. *Dialogue with Trypho*. Translated by Thomas B. Falls. Washington, DC: Catholic University of America Press, 2003.

- Ladd, George Eldon. *The Presence of the Future: The Eschatology of Biblical Realism*. Grand Rapids: Eerdmans, 1974.

- Lindsey, Hal. *The Late Great Planet Earth*. Grand Rapids: Zondervan, 1970.

- Luther, Martin. *Commentary on Galatians*. Translated by Theodore Graebner. Grand Rapids: Zondervan, 1949.

- Luther, Martin. *That Jesus Christ Was Born a Jew*. Translated by Martin H. Bertram. In *Luther's Works*, vol. 45. Philadelphia: Fortress Press, 1962.

- Origen. *Homilies on Jeremiah*. In *The Fathers of the Church*, vol. 97, translated by John Clark Smith. Washington, DC: Catholic University of America Press, 1998.

- Robertson, O. Palmer. *The Christ of the Covenants*. Phillipsburg: Presbyterian and Reformed Publishing, 1980.

- Ryrie, Charles C. *Dispensationalism Today*. Chicago: Moody Press, 1965.

- Scofield, Cyrus I. *The Scofield Reference Bible*. New York: Oxford University Press, 1909.

- Sizer, Stephen. *Christian Zionism: Road-map to Armageddon?* Downers Grove: InterVarsity Press, 2004.

- Soulen, R. Kendall. *The God of Israel and Christian Theology.* Minneapolis: Fortress Press, 1996.

- Tapie, Matthew A. *Aquinas on Israel and the Church: The Question of Supersessionism in the Theology of Thomas Aquinas.* Eugene: Pickwick Publications, 2014.

- Tertullian. *Adversus Judaeos.* In *Ante-Nicene Fathers*, vol. 3, edited by Alexander Roberts and James Donaldson. Peabody: Hendrickson Publishers, 1994.

- Vlach, Michael J. *Has the Church Replaced Israel? A Theological Evaluation.* Nashville: B&H Academic, 2010.

- Weber, Timothy P. *On the Road to Armageddon: How Evangelicals Became Israel's Best Friend.* Grand Rapids: Baker Academic, 2004.

- Wright, N.T. *Jesus and the Victory of God.* Minneapolis: Fortress Press, 1996.

- Wright, N.T. *Paul and the Faithfulness of God.* Minneapolis: Fortress Press, 2013.

- Younger, K. Lawson, Jr. *Ancient Conquest Accounts: A Study in Ancient Near Eastern and Biblical History Writing.* Sheffield: JSOT Press, 1990.

www.ingramcontent.com/pod-product-compliance
Lightning Source LLC
Chambersburg PA
CBHW060846050426
42453CB00008B/852